Aligning CORPORATE LIFECYCLES *and* PRODUCT LIFECYCLES

DR. R. N. GIVHAN

authorHOUSE®

AuthorHouse™
1663 Liberty Drive
Bloomington, IN 47403
www.authorhouse.com
Phone: 1-800-839-8640

Published by AuthorHouse 05/28/2014

ISBN: 978-1-4969-1583-2 (sc)
ISBN: 978-1-4969-1582-5 (e)

Library of Congress Control Number: 2014909768

CONTENTS

Introduction vii

Chapter 1   Theorists 1
      Engineering Management 1
            Engineering management definition 1
            Application 2
      Organizational Impacts 4
            Organizational structure 4
            Integrated organizations 5
            Organizational skills and operation 6
      Engineering Life Cycle Costing 8
            Definition of life cycle cost 8
            Development of life cycle cost 8
      Engineering System Development 15
            Foundation of engineering development 15
                  System development processes 15
                  Engineering quality and system processes 17
      Conclusion 18

Chapter 2   Engineering Management Implementations across Industries 19

Chapter 3   What Does This Mean to My Corporation? 25
      Engineering Management 25
            Engineering management past 26
            Engineering management present 28
      Engineering Management Processes 34
            Organizational and system design applications. 34
            Organizational applications 34
            System development applications 35
            Program management applications 37
      Business Applications 39
      Conclusion 40

Chapter 4   Methods and Implementation 42

    Background 42

    Product Life Cycle Cost and Time to Market 44

        Strategic Model Implementations 45

    Implementation 46

        Business Strategic Development 46

        Engineering Management Life Cycle Cost 49

            Project organization lifecycle 49

            Corporation lifecycle 51

        Product Lifecycle Cost 63

            Product development cost 63

            Product production cost 64

            Operation and retirement cost 65

    Organization Influences 66

Chapter 5   Let's Talk About It 68

Reference 73

INTRODUCTION

Corporations are continuously looking to improve market position and brand. Most limit their evaluations to their current portfolios. Yet, in many cases new product have to be developed to gain the extended market. The book is segmented in to 3 major areas. These are an in-depth understanding theoretically, active application of theory, and a functional application. Some of the major contributor concepts discussed originated from W. Dale Compton, Balbir S. Dhillon, Roger Miller, and Frederick W. Taylor. Each contributed to the fundamentally concepts of engineering management. The theorists' contributions are centered on three areas in reference to the main objectives of this document. The theorists concepts evaluated: (a) the basic management concepts each introduced relative to engineering management, (b) the focus areas of engineering management, and (c) the organizational affects of the concepts. Each theorist provided similar management approaches, yet procedurally their system structure and process are different. This Breadth component has three major objectives. The objectives of this breadth component are to analyze the systematic theories in terms of engineering management regarding its underlying principles, to compare and contrast the philosophies of engineering management in terms of approach methods, and to discuss the strengths and limitations on discussed applications of engineering management applications in various systematic approaches.

The theorists provided comprehensive detail about the development of management and the applicability of management to engineering projects. They introduced the relationships that exist between cost, management, and quality. Each theorist used meaningful examples to describe the practical approached to managing the creation of designing and building a product. From baseline theory additional manufacturing system theories developed methods for applying business and organizational processes to the management of manufactured products. Management methods described by each theorist strongly focused on the organizations, infrastructure integration, and structured cost of the processes. The relationships of cost and quality provide illustrate areas of focus for management personnel. The company leaders used the theories discussed to build comprehensive implementation strategies for company success. The structure of the organization dictated the implementation of processes, such as goal and objective development. The theorist recognizes and discusses psychology philosophies of organizational implementation and in the development of engineering management systems. These over-arching themes provide a holistic approach for managing engineering projects. The management of such items required overseeing from conception to replacement product. Within these processes, the evolution of new products with structured cost needs requires management knowledge and forward thinking. The process of implementation created by these theorists has become standard procedure for many industries. Templates provided by these theorists give insight into statistical control needs of the organization.

CHAPTER 1

Theorists

ENGINEERING MANAGEMENT

Fredrick Taylor brought to light a phenomenon taking place in manufacturing environments across America in the beginning stages of product development. This phenomenon was the struggle between employee and employer in factories. To Taylor, the structured system in vogue at the time seemed to create a misalignment of employer objectives and employee objectives (Taylor, 1967). Based on his analysis of this situation, Taylor proposed new philosophies in methods management could use to improve company profitability and productivity (Taylor, 1967). This phase in time contributed to the American Industrial Age after World War I by introducing methods for manufacturing and organizational development that centered on product manufacturing. This new development created a need for a cross pollination of business skills and engineering skills.

Engineering management definition. The initial philosophy of Engineering Management developed from the concepts Taylor introduced. Taylor's method removed the concepts of rule of thumb and provided management with a task oriented method for production. Taylor created the theory of scientific management on a basis that the management structures develop systems of task management and employee management. These are the beginning steps for Engineering Management (Compton, 1997).

The introduction of technical applications within manufacturing is the next level with engineering management. Compton (1969) highlighted the infusion of finical support from governmental agencies moves manufacturing and various industries to greater levels of knowledge and structure system development. In contrast to Taylor, Compton suggested the terminology of traditional knowledge and scientific management become rephrased as "applied research, advanced development, development, production engineering, manufacturing engineering, and manufacturing" (Compton, 1969, p. 3). This due greatly to physicist of the 1940s moving in environments structured for solving engineering problems. These terms became the norm of large industrial companies like Ford and General Motors. Within a twenty-year evolution of the sciences, the National Academy of Engineering was born (Compton, 1969). The usage of the terms became synonymous with technical task and work. To broaden the practice intense levels of training became the requirement (Compton, 1969). This training contributed to the development of scientific solutions to technical problems (Compton, 1969). The presence of such process in solution development and research initiatives expand the definition of engineering (Compton, 1969). The management of engineering aligned to Compton's statement that man may be the controller of technology or controlled by technology (1969). Within this process, evolutionary concepts of engineering and management require broader knowledge of then considered independent systems.

Dhillon's (1987) approach moved the definition engineering management initially into different segments. Moving away from the manufacturing focus of Compton, Dhillon (1987) defined management as being comprised of three elements. Dhillon stated "It is the process of work that involves guiding a class of persons to accomplish stated organizational objectives" (1987, p. 3). The three elements are resources, which include funding and workers; manage activities, and business goals (1987). Dhillon highlighted that engineering management concepts evolve from engineers moving into management roles and focuses on productivity and efficiencies. Dhillon (1987, p. 9) stated "40 percent of industrial executives are from engineering backgrounds." The foundation of this process began in the analysis of Taylor. During early 1900s, Taylor recognized that most managers were former artisan or formal trained/educated engineers (1911). Taylor evens suggested using gangster bosses as leadership role models (1911). Taylor summarized the commanding skills and strong presence of such individuals aids in the execution of task management (1911). Dhillon (1987) highlighted that many engineers moving into management roles attend business schools to develop management skills. Dhillon (1987, p. 33) defined engineering management as "a discipline which fulfills the need of an engineering manager because it is the intersection of engineering and management."

Taylor's, Compton, and Dhillon provide application detail in their definitions, while Miller approached the concept focusing in established organizations. Miller's (2000) approach to engineering management is an expansive sense relating to the strategic implementation of large engineering projects. Miller (2000) emphasized methods for integrated responsibility in the development of the product. Miller (2000) established concepts of arrangements between government entities, entrepreneurs, and rational systems, which were established based on management evolutions and strategic coordination between competitors. Each demonstrated the evolution of the field engineering management and its broad application.

Application. In Taylor's analysis mostly industrial environments, consist of many job skills delivered through family teachings and observation (1967). Within each communication, streamlining of process and creativity for shortcuts produced systematic competition. Taylor's analysis of the methods and elimination of antiquated processes did not take place (1967). Taylor deemed this information as 'traditional knowledge'. Compton highlighted these individuals as Artisans (1997). Knowledge extracted from the act of artisans. Generally this information was communicated intra family or apprentice positions (Compton, 1997). The artisan positions controlled the work therefore developing mastery attitude within the workers (Taylor, 1967). Taylor highlighted that it is the responsibility of management to draw knowledge and excellence out of the worker (1967). Taylor suggested creating programs that provide recognition opportunities to the workers to get the most work possible accomplished (1967). Taylor further offered management methods to build a scientific process for controlling and evolving traditional knowledge (1967). This evolution of task in specific formats and with time constraint demonstrates the scientific analysis of such task. Taylor stated "It is the combination of the initiative of the workmen, coupled with the new types of work done be the management, that makes scientific management so much more efficient that the old plan" (1967,

p. 37). Taylor's foundational analysis of management and task provided industrial institution with methods for production of product. This foundation established by Taylor introduced uniformity in manufacturing during the industrial industry beginnings. Fundamentally, Dhillon and Compton extracted concepts from Taylor leaving virtually minor areas of evolution in their terms defining Engineering Management. Using Taylor's scientific methods large industries were able to grow in profitability and business structure (Taylor, 1967). In the evolution of manufacturing technical influenced, drive the industry into a new generation of process and development.

Similarly, Taylor and Compton believe businesses management required a different set of skills. Compton emphasized that engineering management are independent roles and segments, as well as Dhillon. Those roles are a management individuals circled by the concepts of organizational structures and leadership development. Compton then included manufacturing concepts related to customer needs (1997). The engineering portion of the process aligned to system development processes and concepts such as "Just-In-Time" manufacturing methods (Compton, 1997). The role of the engineer focused on product development for customer delivery. Compton segmented manufacturing into independent processes used only in manufacturing (1997). Compton related the management of the system to the vertical integration of the organization (1997). Compton placed the two entities into very different categories (1997).

Engineering management from each theorist focuses on various aspects of engineering management. While Dhillon proposed the significance of engineering management centers around the background and education of the manager, Compton (1997) segregated the concepts of engineering and management. Compton isolated management activities to the organization and describes product-manufacturing processes as engineering responsibilities (1997). These processes have management over sight, yet individuals in management roles are not considered engineering individuals (Compton, 1997). Compton presented manufacturing management methods such as queuing and event analysis (1997). The management oversight Compton described has no requirement to be engineering trained. Taylor created the foundation of product production and management placing focus on the responsibilities of management (1911). Taylor dictated management's understanding of the manual task must be in place for sequencing and labor analysis (1911). Taylor acknowledged that most people in the role of management are former workers with additional training (1967). These individuals understand the traditional knowledge of the workmanship and the objects of management (1911). These processes contribute to the engineering opportunities in development. Dhillon aligned with Taylor emphasizing management's knowledge base and skills expanding to beyond that of just engineering (1987). In further analysis, Miller's (2000) consideration of engineering management extended to contract management, risk management, arrangement and relationship management required by large programs. Miller (2000) described the roles of individuals involved in the process are engineers. Miller stated that decisions within the design, development, relationships, and arrangements require engineering skills and training (2000). In this process, engineers are tasked with creating product development plans and selecting contract supplier proposals (Miller, 2000). Miller (2000) highlighted the development of partnerships in contractual agreements in the creation of product.

With the evolution of technology, production processes, and market impacts, the role of the engineering manager expands. The complexity of products, suppliers, and information development increased the network of resources and applications managed. In many ways, engineering management became an umbrella of skills linking engineering knowledge with that of business applications and skills.

ORGANIZATIONAL IMPACTS

In any corporate environment, the organizational structure has a strong impact on the production, profitability, and growth of the company. The organizational structure aligned to job task and business unit producibility. The hierarchical structure demonstrated the level at which decision making takes place. An organizational hierarchy can be a centralized system or a decentralized system. In the creation of product the organizational decision, development of processes has a high impact to the product processes within the manufacturing, engineering, and other integrations to the organization. Each theorist approached the development of organizational structures in various ways.

Organizational structure. Such analysis of the organization is an imperative to the work of Taylor. Taylor stated that in the development of systematic task management, managers have four additional tasks beyond that of monitoring workers (1967). The first of these tasks required that management create knowledge of what workers or artisans actual manufacture (Taylor, 1967). This process in a general sense required the manager to have clear definition of the job itself (Taylor, 1967). This scientific method used to examine segmented work activities produces incremental phasing for management's involvement and task completeness. In creating an organization, Taylor suggested using a more simplified environment (1911). Secondly, Taylor emphasized that large engineering organizations may be to intricate to manage for timing analysis of the simplified task (1911). Taylor emphasized the importance of having talented leadership, which is the third activity (1911). Taylor recognized organizational structures configurations are similar to the military hierarchical structure and establishes control over the worker (Taylor, 1911). This required a specific type of leadership and distinct skill. Fourth of these task, Taylor suggested by no longer using the military hierarchy the organization structure can subdivide the work for better planning (1911). Due to the input of Taylor, his methods are known to be fundamental to organization structures and organizational development. Taylor also provided concepts based in how many functional people verse non-functional people. Taylor stated,

> In the case of a company doing a manufacturing business with a uniform and simple product for the maximum economy, the number of producers to each non-producer would of course be larger. No manager need feel alarmed then when he sees the number of non-producers increasing in proportion to producers, providing the non-producers are busy all their time, and providing, of course, that in each case they are doing efficient work. (Taylor, 1911, p. 1406)

Taylor's analysis of functional and non-functional role evolved to integrated organizations. The cross-functional applications of the additional organizations developed the initial needs of the entire corporation.

Similarly, in the evolution of organizational structures, manufacturing, and product creation, these components are drivers to developing holistic management systems (Compton, 1997). The organizational structure and hierarchical implementation have concepts introduced by Henry R. Towne and others (Compton, 1997). Structure systems for strategic development and achievement of system goals are fundamental inputs to the hierarchical structure of the organization (Compton, 1997) aligning to Taylor's approach in understanding the task of the workers. The development of strategic business goals and market analysis became the system terms (Compton, 1997). Compton stated, "Operational goals and objectives relate to the general operating objectives that an enterprise has established, as well as the specific goals that an enterprise has for its products, services, and processes" (1997, p. 71). Such that Compton's approach to engineering management is similar in concept to that of standard management, practice implementations embraced today and created by Taylor. The organization sub-levels should have lower level goals that loop back into to the operations overall goals. Taylor's approach provided the foundation for Dhillon where organizational structured take on a different appearance in relation to purpose and job skill need within the analysis of Dhillon (1987). This concept aligned to the removal of the military hierarchy Taylor suggested. Dhillon suggested organizational methods for structuring the hierarchy (1987). From a variety of sources, Dhillon highlighted the use of functional, product, project and torrential organizational structures (1987). A distinctly different approach from Dhillon or Compton is Miller's organizational reflection. The term organization has a different meaning and representation for the concepts Miller introduces. Miller (2000) described organizations as entities of professional activities. The organizations Miller referenced were government agencies and public corporate systems (2000). Miller demonstrated the inactions of these entities. Miller emphasized the flow of work and decision between the entities (2000). Miller stated that in the development of large engineering projects there are many responsible persons (2000). Miller highlighted the desire to identify, understand, and assign positions. Within the development of the engineering project, involvement roles and responsibilities of during the workflow of the overall program are important success measures (2000). Miller suggested such processes assist in determining program risk and within independent entities (2000). Miller's approach allowed the agencies to understand workflow and interrelationship needs. Miller does not focus on the details of the lower levels; more appropriately aligned the structure with the development and needs of the product. The baseline creations of Taylor evolve into concepts both Compton and Dhillon develop. Miller moved the method to a high-level analysis.

Integrated organizations. The structured silos of organizations developed during the initial stages of the industrial age followed the example of government agencies (Dhillon, 2002). In the development of task management Taylor illustrated the integrated processing that occurred (1911). Taylor's process suggested having representation from all functional and non-functional organizations indentified having a specific task (1911). Taylor provided examples of departments for a specific organization such as messenger system, employee bureau, and push order department (1911). The push order department provided mail and delivery services to the organization (Taylor, 1911). Each department provided the organization with specific functional skill. Taylor (1911) even suggested assigning a man to evaluate areas of improvement. Comparably, Compton suggested the usage of benchmarking, which is the discovery of process practices proven to the best in industry (1997). Benchmarking is a business management term (1997). Benchmarking required the process analysis in comparison to the process performance (Compton, 1997). Compton suggested integrating business skill and process in the development of product (1997). In the analysis of marketing process, Compton suggested the usage of detail finical analysis and metric analysis. Dhillon's approach included combination organization using a term such as matrix (2002). Dhillon defined matrix organizations as functional and project concepts networked (2002). Dhillon suggested that engineering work segments create functional organizes (1987). These integrations are inclusive of many organizations. Compton only discussed limited organizational integrations with business Dhillon expanded the philosophy. Dhillon further described the advantages and disadvantages to structuring organizations in these formats (1987). Dhillon suggested the flow of data and communication improves by having such organizations (1987). Akin to the low-level integrations, Miller focused the entire development of the project on integrating organizations (2000). Miller's approach included the integration of government entities with private sectors businesses for product development (2000). Compendiously, we evaluate the evolution of integrations from Taylor to Dhillon. The basis resided in the development of the organization, product, and the customer needs.

Organizational skills and operation. With the creation of any organization, evaluation of skills may drive the hierarchy of the structure. In the development of production organizations, specific skills were identified prior to any structure development. Taylor focused on two main areas of skill, which are the production workers artisan and leadership. The leadership skills, which Taylor identifies, are as follows:

- Brains
- Education
- Special or technical knowledge; manual dexterity or strength
- Tact
- Energy
- Grit
- Honesty
- Judgment or common sense
- Good Health (Taylor, 1911, p. 1389)

Taylor continued to highlight leadership personnel should be technically capable to be considered for those positions. Taylor's suggested hiring leadership with multiple skills listed above. Taylor stated,

> The fact that plenty of men can be had who combine four or five of these attributes, it becomes evident that the work of management should be so subdivided that the various positions can be filled by men of this caliber, and great part of the art of management undoubtedly lies in planning the work this way. (1911, p. 1390)

Dhillon specifically focused on the needs of engineers within the process of organizational development (1987). According to Dhillon, an engineer required the following:

- Job security with respect to his or her attainments
- Proper work facilities
- Necessary technical assistance
- Stimulating and challenging work
- Taking part in those decisions which will affect him or her
- Adequate supporting staff
- Bosses who are competent
- Recognition for his or her work from management

- Economic advancement
- Proper work assignments
- Opportunities for self-development
- Employment with an organization which has clearly defined responsibilities and authority
- Employment with a reputable organization
- Work variety
- Chance of his or her ideas being practiced
- Independence to attack a work problem (Dhillon, 1987, pp. 33-32).

Dhillon (1987) proposed methods for advancing engineer's career paths and promotions to management. Dhillon highlighted specific items to motivate engineering staff. Dhillon spotlights the engineer as a major role (1987). Dhillon detailed the psychological needs of the engineer. Dhillon documented how to manage the engineer. Dhillon considered other staff yet in various roles. Dhillon's approached seems to focus the need for handling engineers in all facets of their individual careers. In the development of the organization, Dhillon also suggested building an environment of innovation. Dhillon provided action that one can take to create an innovative environment. These environments are in alignment to the engineer and manager roles. In creating these environments, Dhillon defined barriers within an organization and introduces technical methods for getting around these barriers. Dhillon (1987) gave valuable insight to developing an organization containing engineering personnel. Both Miller and Compton identify skills necessary for management processes and process management. The individual needs and capabilities are in alignment only to the hierarchical requirements for product development.

The internal functioning of the organization depends greatly on the individual organizational applications. Dhillon described the human or psychology side of management in dealing with human needs (1987). In an overall approach, Compton recognized the requirement to address the psychological needs of the individual as part of the development of the organization (1997). These activities demonstrated roles within the management structure (Compton, 1997). Compton also described concepts of employee involvement and employee engagement drawing and the need to have all levels of the organizational structure involved in business strategy, goals, and objective development. The empowerment of employees allows any level employee the opportunity to introduce process improvements (Compton, 1997). Compton even suggested a corporate change model to move organizations in the direction of open communication (1997). Compton emphasized many strategies for employee satisfaction and performance evaluation processes (1997). All areas leading back to the employee position in the organizational structure (Compton, 1997). Miller in contrast made no mention of these aspects of the organizations and the development of product.

Dhillon (2002) expanded the development of engineering organizations in his next body of work. Dhillon provided more detail in creating engineering departments. Dhillon provided functional activities as well as organizational strategic objectives. Dhillon's approach detailed the organizational requirements based on having engineering personnel. Dhillon's approach even defined how conference rooms should be furnished and organized to have efficient meetings with engineers. Dhillon detailed organizational efficiencies by defining algorithms to determine the number of reports an organization creates yearly. Dhillon's algorithm analyzed employee output about the organizational size (2002).

In final analysis, each theorist defined organizational structuring very differently. Each highlights components of the organization. The focus areas are actual structure and hierarchy, job skill, and finally individuals. Dhillon provided tremendous detail on the creation of an Engineering Organization using both standard and specific processes aligned to the skill of engineering. Where Compton communicated organizational structures based on the standard organizational processes. Compton did not define specific roles. Compton, using many philosophies developed by organizational specialist, described organizational development focusing on organization goals and objectives. Compton also focused on individual participation within the organization, which includes leadership. Compton drove that development of the organization to the customer level. Miller completely structures his communication around the fact organizations are in place. Miller's references to organizations are specific to structured entities. Each approach consists of important factors to create successful projects and organizations. Each emphasized networked communication and structure design approaches, which are value added concepts.

ENGINEERING LIFE CYCLE COSTING

In managing engineering projects, the concepts of cost structures and employee processes are factors in developing a successful plan. The development of organizational hierarchical structures aligned with functional application and cost to create the most lean and efficient programs. The concept of managing engineering projects aligns to managing the cost of the projects. An effort to evolve the concept of continuous improvement drove organizations to re-align, restructure, and even remove functions within the structure.

Definition of life cycle cost. During the times of Taylor, there were minimal applications to understanding the systems of cost. During this time cost allocations centered on specific areas of labor and standard business cost. Taylor's approach in developing scientific management focuses on cost associated with manufacturing. Taylor's (1911) approach aids in creating system of manufacturing, where high quality and lower labor cost were the outputs. Dhillon extracted data from a 1971 analysis conducted by the Logistics Management Institute. The output is a summary report producing the Department of Defense directive 5000.1 entitled Acquisition of Major Defense Systems. This directive is in use today, yet it is DoD Directive 5000.5. From the analysis of Untied States Government the concept of life cycle costs, begin. The document created the governmental requirement that all major defense purchases complete life cycle costing. According to Dhillon, life cycle cost is "the sum of all costs incurred during the life time of an item, i.e., the total of procurement and ownership cost" (1989, p 3). Where Compton defined life cycle cost in reference to concurrent engineering processes, and therefore states the goal for an interdisciplinary team is "to accomplish a design that will provide a product that has the desired attributes, that can easily be manufactured and serviced, and that will meet the quality and cost objectives that have been established" (1997, p 274). Miller seemed to align life cycle cost with risk management and the cost associated with mitigating those risks. Dhillon's analysis is a holistic view, where Compton and Miller evaluated specific aspects that contribute to the cost of a product. Products have costs to develop, costs to produce, and costs to maintain.

Development of life cycle cost. The term life cycle is synonymous with business and engineering development programs. The complete development of a product requires consideration of the life cycle of the item. Taylor's approach to production allows the industry to indentify cost areas and cost needs (1911). Through this process, Taylor was able to increase the pay of the workers in his job area. Taylor's system contributed to the life cost in the following ways:

- The method improves quality
- Reduces wasted materials during manufacturing
- Reduces employee dissatisfaction – labor relation cost.

By understanding the work process and define the training need Taylor proved that his method of task management contribute to improving the company's bottom line (1911). Taylor demonstrated that task management is essential to improving the profit of the company (1911). Taylor stated that "in the face of the self-evident fact that maximum prosperity can exist only as the result of the determined effort if each workman turn out each day his largest possible day's work," (1911, pp. 9-10) demonstrating the activity of the worker contributed to the overall cost of the product. Taylor demonstrated methods for developing cost for manufacturing a product in the planning list he created:

- The complete analysis of all orders for machines or work taken by the company.
- Time study for all work done by hand throughout the works, including that done in setting the work in machines, and all bench, vise work and transportation, etc.
- Time study for all operations done by the various machines.
- The balance of, all materials, raw materials, stores and finished parts, and the balance of the work ahead for each class of machines and workmen.
- The analysis of all inquiries for new work received in the sales department and promises for time of delivery.
- The cost of all items manufactured with complete expense analysis and complete monthly comparative cost and expense exhibits.
- The pay department.
- The Mnemonic Symbol System for identification of parts and for charges.
- Information bureau.
- Standards.
- Maintenance of system and plant, and use of the tickler.
- Messenger system and post office delivery.
- Employment bureau.
- The shop disciplinarian.
- A mutual accident insurance association.
- Rush order department.
- Improvement of system or plant. (Taylor, 1911, p. 1399)

By using the above list, Taylor identified all of the expected cost (1911). Taylor evolved the steps to include detail information about material purchase and designing activities (1911). In the list above, Taylor specifically determined the operations required to finish the product and the line path it would follow based on the Mnemonic Symbol System (1911). Even in the in developing the steps for the task Taylor state,

> In fixing the times for the task, and the piece-work rates in jobs of this class, the job should be subdivided into a number of divisions, and a separate time and price assigned to each division rather than to assign a single time and price for the whole job. (Taylor, 1911, p. 1380)

These processes contributed to the development of Dhillon's approach to cost. Dhillon identified some costs that contribute to the life cycle cost as the following:

- Purchase Cost –moneys invested in or use to acquire the items
- Ownership Cost – moneys used to maintain and replace items
    - Maintenance Cost – product labor etc. required to maintain item
    - Recurring Cost – moneys payable cyclical during the life of the item
    - Failure Cost – moneys lost due to the failure of the item during assumed work hours
    - Reliability Cost – money paid due to unmet reliability percentages
    - Repair Cost –moneys paid to repair the item
- Manufacturing Cost –money or investment required to manufacture the item
- Non-recurring Cost- single cost pay out cost (1989).

The analysis of these cost provide a total item or product cost (1989). Additional cost may be included, the basis of such cost definitions align to the business structure and business need.

Dhillon (1989) highlighted various specific cost data requirements and identifies that business, management; development, reliability; manufacturing and maintenance are drivers of cost. Dhillon's approach analyzed the business aspect of the product. Dhillon determined models necessary to understand the initial investment to development product. Dhillon emphasized that economic environments contribute to the cost structure of the product. In many cases the economic cost align to corporate lending or available invest moneys the corporation may need to contribute. These funds are useful in start-up development cost. In many of the economic models, Dhillon examined the future worth, present worth, and depreciation cost of the items development (1989).

Dhillon (1989) described steps used by various analysts in the development of life cycle cost. The fundamental synergies center on the following concepts:

- understand the usages of the product and determine product life usefulness
- determine cost of manufacturing the items, including manufacture environment set-up etc., material
- cost of maintaining the items based on estimated usages and usefulness
- determine product development recurring cost
- evaluate present worth of the product
- evaluate termination cost for the item
- determine discount cost (Dhillon, 1989).

Some areas not reflected in Dhillon's structure are design cost beyond that of mechanical engineering, such as software development (1989). Considerations of software during these engineering years are recurring cost and not analyzed as a complete product. Comparative analysis against previous programs allowed the reviewer to complete a general estimate of required cost for the purchase of the product (Dhillon, 1989). Dhillon suggested by completing life cycle costing product goals and objectives are achievable by creating a detail management plan (1989). Dhillon (1989) recommended applying the same techniques in using suppliers. In the process of developing request for proposals requirements flowed down to the supplier in the development of the contracted product aid in solidifying the upstream cost incurred by the prime contractor or customer. Dhillon (1989) provided three life cycle cost models, which are Heuristic models, Conceptual models, and Analytical models. There are sub-levels to these models that Dhillon (1989) highlighted providing additional detail to the cost structure. The sub-level for the analytical model is total cost models, design trade model, and logistics support models. Dhillon (1989) further segregated life cycle cost to be both specific and non-specific. Dhillon (1989) identified ten non-specific life cycle cost models that are applicable to any in format not specific to a product. Dhillon (1989) also provided thirteen specific life cycle cost models applicable to a specific product. The specific models have variables associated with specific components such as a motor or system hardware (Dhillon, 1989). The specific models required more detail historical and functional data to quantify the true cost (Dhillon, 1989). The non-specific life cycle cost aligned more to software products generally during that time (Dhillon, 1989). As software developments are more specific in requirements development etc. today it aligned with a more specific life cycle cost structure (Dhillon, 1989). Dhillon (1989) further provided costing development techniques that support your individual environment. Dhillon (1989) defined in detail manufacturing cost, as well as, reliability and maintenance cost techniques. Dhillon's approach to system cost is inclusive of every phase of product development (1989). The structured models provide engineering and business management with a structured approach to understanding company expenses.

The creation of product requires management to be involved with understanding all associated cost. Compton (1997) had taken a slightly different approach to development of life cycle cost. Compton (1997) began his analysis of cost with that of the product market and development. Compton (1997) suggested product analysis centered on system introduction into the market and saturation of the market. Where Dhillon cost analysis focused on governmental applications, Compton aligned to commercial applications such as computer system etc. (1997). Compton identifies the logistics growth function as a method to understand market needs and develop strategic objectives (1997). Compton (1997) provided limited information on specific system cost structures. Compton (1997) focused on design methodologies for quality improvements. Compton (1997) also focused on operations and manufacturing processes with little reflection of cost in applying such processes. Compton actually has very little data on identifying product cost systems (1997).

In many environments, technologies are research projects, which involve areas that many designers, developers, and management personnel have little to no data collected about the technology. Therefore, Miller's risk management detailed adds value to understanding new technology development. Miller on a macroscopic level aligns with Dhillon and aspects of Compton's process. Concepts that Miller (2000) introduced with partnerships and arrangements segment the costs to a component level. The segregated components created individual cost structures aligning to internal system development. The internal development of the systems involves the agreement within the arrangements who and where technical, management, etc. cost are paid. Risk definition according to Miller are "the possibility that events, the resulting impacts, the associated actions and the dynamic interactions among the three may turn out differently as anticipated" (2000, p.76). Miller suggested the usage of Gaussian approach to understanding the outcomes risk involved. Miller (2000) structured stated applying the process of risk management to cost needs. In lower-levels of the cost analysis are not discussed by Miller, yet it is evident processes similar to that of Dhillon are useful. Miller's focuses for risk analysis are governmental agencies, which are the entities used to create Dhillon's detail evaluations of costs.

> Manager, however, not only are interested in the variability of returns but they pay attention to the drivers of risks that are likely to affect future project performance. From a managerial perspective, uncertainty is ignorance of the true stated of nature and the causal structures of decision issues. Weak uncertainty holds when, managers have enough information to structure problems, estimate distribution, and build decision models. Strong uncertainty characterizes situations in which there is such an absence of knowledge and information that decision-making issues are ambiguous. (Miller, 2000, p. 76)

Miller identified types of risk that apply to the life cycle of a product. The risk Miller highlighted are as following (2000):

- Market Related Risk
  - Market Risk – risk identified based on various system forecast project needs and understanding supply and demand within the market
  - Financial Risk – risk identified in relationship to institutional contributions from investors etc.
  - Supply Risk – risk identified in relationship to accessibility and acquiring needed materials
- Completion Risk
  - Technical Risk – risk identified that align to engineering issues and difficulties
  - Construction Risk – risk identified that highlight issues of manufacturability
  - Operational Risk – risk identified that focus on manufacturing systems or equipment needs
- Institutional Risk
  - Regulatory Risk – risk identified to control contractual agreements and associations between subcontractors etc.
  - Social-acceptability Risk – risk identified associated with environment and community affiliations in where the product is created and terminated
  - Sovereign Risk – risk identified are governmental and propriety requirements that may change during the life of the product

All contributing to product overall cost structure. Miller (2000) suggested effective risk management contributed to product success by examining long-term benefits. Miller emphasized that risk management evolves security in finical gains established by the project's development (2000). Other cost concepts identified by Millers make use of strategic template applications.

Miller emphasized strategic system and templates created to expand business capabilities (2000). Miller discussed templates established by the International Program in the Management of Engineering and Construction (2000). These templates create opportunity for foreign nations in the establishment of projects. For many international programs, the templates provide insight to system financing and governmental involvements. Areas covered in the template are listed below: (Miller, 2000, p. 117)

Table 1.
Templates used in IMEC projects

Financial	Nonrecourse project financing
	Public placement of bonds
	Credit Grading be rating agencies
	Risk –analysis seminars
Ownership	Alliances of partners
	Power purchase agreement –Build operate transfer agreements concession
	Repowering
	Entrepreneurial projects independent power plant
Contract	Turnkey contracting
	Round table decisions
	Design-finance-build-contract
	Frame supply agreement
Organizational	Participatory engineering
	Continuous commissioning
	Partnering with contractors-suppliers
	Coengineering in the design with suppliers
Legitimacy	Codefinition with regulator
	Public-private partnerships
	Mutual-gains approach
	State Agreements

Miller's approached to large projects are a summation of the listed factors above (2000). Miller included cost drivers developed in the late 80s for product development. These are new areas to consider in establishing system life cycle cost. In some cases, the application of such cost may contribute to non-recurring cost detailed by Dhillon. The requirements in creating an engineering program are more inclusive of international influences in today's market. Miller also spoke of program incentives as additional program cost controls (2000). Miller argued that in the allocation of risk, cost may rise for the contractor. The agreement of responsibility and authority may increase the programs cost. These increases may contribute to the success of the project or the failure of the project. Miller explained the detail in appropriately allocating risk (2000).

The goal is to allocate responsibility for dealing with a certain risk to the participant deemed to have the most adequate combination of skills, resources, control, information, and risk-bearing capacity. Incentives are designed to trigger appropriate behavior. For instance, if a contractor is awarded a contract with a fixed cost and a certain delivery date, but must pay liquidated damages in case of nonperformance, the completion risk for the agreed scope of the contract is allocated his solution creates new risk, however, stemming from the loss of direct control by the owner. (Miller, 2000, p.125)

These additional costs align to life cycle cost in the design, development, manufacturing and delivery of the product from the contractor (Miller, 2000). The contractor may not expect low performance on the part of their internal resources. These cost contribute to profit lose in the development of the product.

Miller (2000) structured an analysis on the process of financing large programs. Miller (2000) stated in the process of acquiring financers the risk involved with creating debt or establishing equity against the program. Miller laid out equity indeed has a higher risk then debt and requires a higher return. Yet, Miller stated within a capital market the adjustments made on both equity and debt are relatively the same. Miller illustrated the return on equity is higher than debt and may increase based on the higher risk assumed in investment, where debt payout are static as defined in the contractual agreement (2000). In any event, the development of risk aligned to development of potential cost evolving from the structured life cycle of the product or system.

The need to evaluate cost for programs from initial concept to final termination of the product is a driver to corporate portfolios. The life cycle of the product includes all related actions during this process. Each product goes through various phase during its evolving life. The cost relationship determined the viability of the product. For many corporations cost questions determine the whether the product will make it to market. In evaluating the theorist, each demonstrated a different perspective of the process. Taylor, as one of the first to consider these concepts demonstrated the value creating methods to move worker to assist in lower cost. The process of training and reward systems motivated worker to effeciently, improve quality, and increase output. This process has relationships to supply and demand. Taylor's approach minimizes cost and improves supply. Concerning Dhillon, a detail analysis of life cost contributed to the large number of system models and method development for application on many systems. Dhillon provided cost methods at every phase of the program. The business strategic evaluation for present worth and future worth aid in stream lining production or system design development cost. Compton's evaluations remain at a high level. Compton's approach to market analysis drew one to think the details for systematic evaluations are available. Compton and Dhillon agreed that systematic views of the product inclusive of business specific analysis are important for decision making in creating new products. Miller's approaches are beyond the preliminary business analysis stage. Miller's approach taken on cost from a more cause and effect process in the development of risk associated to the product. The costs of the risk during the various phases contributed to the bottom line life cycle cost. Miller does though focused on agreements and arrangements where cost may align to entities following the contractual understandings. By synthesizing, the methods each contribute to expanding the understanding application of life cycle cost.

ENGINEERING SYSTEM DEVELOPMENT

The process for managing engineering systems began with the understanding engineering system development. Engineering systems development process are inclusive of initial conception evaluations to manufacturing the product. The development philosophies evolve based on what types of system are needed. Dhillon, Compton, Taylor, and Miller provided specific views of such process from various positions.

Foundation of engineering development. During the industrial revolution, the theories of Taylor are fundamental. In many ways, Taylor's Scientific Management processes are the foundation of both Dhillon and Compton's philosophies. Taylor described method for executing task developed by an artisan. Taylor's approach examined the task involved in the manufacturing of the product, where duration and complexity were measured. Taylors's process created a systematic analysis to how manufacturing completes a job. Taylor structured the task in the most effective and efficient order to maximize time to completion. Taylor demonstrated the creation of plans aligned to these task and the best methods to complete the plans successfully. A part of this process, Taylor acknowledged the worth of the worker and provides methods to control the efforts of the worker. Taylor's philosophies became the fundamental system development process. In developing theories of today, Compton, Dhillon and Miller extracted from the work of Taylor. Compton's use of Taylor begins with task duration and planning (1911). Taylor's process for subdividing task allowed the planning to be more specific (1911). This process allowed the task to be repeatable and aids in the production of best practices. Dhillon's approach began with the history and methods of Taylor demonstrating the evolution of process based on the evolution of technology. Miller's approach aligned his task integration implementation, which included organizational levels of full agencies.

System development processes. Manufacture and production are within the final phases of engineering system development. Manufacturing and production staged are major components of Compton's contribution (1997). Compton's contributing philosophies involved the integration of manufacturing systems and planning systems. In the development of an integrated process, Compton states the institutions teach a very linear process in the development of a product (1988). Compton suggested the linearity causes rework and bad decisions (1988). Compton provided a more inclusive process in the design phase of a product (1988). Similarly, Dhillon embraced an expanded process inclusive of system engineering phases and design engineering phases in the development of products (1996). Compton believed the design process should have levels of task, which include functional design, manufacturing, and life cycle consideration (1988). Compton's approach is very specific to hardware electrical engineering design and mechanical system design (1997). During the functional phase, Compton highlighted the selection of materials completed by the design engineer (1988). Compton's suggestion is to integrate activities of the manufacturing engineer, functional engineer, as well as other business services such as finance (1997). To expand the life cycle philosophy Compton introduced the manufacturing life cycle, which has its own defined phases (1988). Compton described the phases are feasibility, aggregate, detail, implementation, ongoing operations, and obsolescence & termination (1988). Each phase proceeded as an analysis phase concerning manufacturing and production. The feasibility analysis phase is the evaluation of the product to determine profit and loss aspects of the product (Compton, 1988). In this phase product comparisons and ratings, determined the decision to move to the next phase of the life cycle (Compton, 1988). The aggregate analysis phase begins once the most feasible product selection is complete (Compton, 1988). The aggregate analysis phase examined the needed configuration for those selected systems (Compton, 1988). The detail analysis phase further down selects the systems approved to move forward (Compton, 1988). This phase created functional applications, production capacity planning, and organizational impacts (Compton, 1988). The implementation phase was the actual implementation of the plan created during the previous phases (Compton, 1988). Once the product is complete, maintenance of the product begins (Compton, 1988). The final phase of usage of the product finish takes place if the product is beyond the obsolescence phase, which is termination (Compton, 1988). During the obsolescence phase any sub components maybe usable for repairing other systems or sub components maybe replace obsolescence individual parts (Compton, 1988). The concurrent process Compton identified is a structure to elimination inefficient communication and link internal processes (1997). Where Dhillon's structured approach included understanding the reason for the design, which leads to evaluating the type of engineering design, may be incorporated. Dhillon defined design types as creative, adaptive, or developmental. Each type of design required the application of specific process design steps (1996). In describing the design process Dhillon structured his development around the works of P. H. Hill. Dhillon emphasized using the following twelve steps:

- Problem identification
- Problem definition
- Information gathering
- Task specification
- Idea generation
- Conceptualization
- Analysis
- Experimentation
- Solution presentation
- Production
- Product distribution
- Consumption (Dhillon, 1996, p. 35).

Each stage Dhillon described enhances the application of the design specifications (1996). Other tasks Dhillon include are design reviews (1996). Dhillon provided a list of engineering personnel necessary to complete the design process (1996). The jobs skills according to Dhillon include are reliability, maintenance, quality, human factors, safety, and manufacturing engineers (1996). Dhillon suggested various mathematical methods to create systematic designs (1996). As listed Dhillon included analysis at each step to understand feasibility, obsolesce, and so forth (1996). Compton included constructs such as evaluations of design manufacturability, usage, functional application, and strategic analysis of assembly of the product for reparability (1988). Compton further analyzed the design processes in developing the entire system (1988). Compton defined design analysis as the decision to design a suggested product and manufacture that product where in a general since design analysis is a period where designs approaches maybe taken into consideration (1988). Compton suggested using product models in making these decisions. Compton's approach excluded the use of system engineering philosophies and focused on the manufacturing efforts of the company, differing completely from that of Dhillon's philosophies.

Engineering quality and system processes. High-level system development required specific inputs for complete product creation. Compton (1997) additionally highlighted quality functions in the process of manufacturing. Compton (1997) suggested implementing customer requirements throughout the full manufacturing life cycle and additional functionally related teams in the organization. These concepts are the foundational application in implementing quality functional deployments. Compton emphasized production control as part of the manufacturing life cycle using applications such as Just-In-Time (JIT) production, Master Schedule production (MRP), and Statistical Process Control (SPC) (1997). Each production supplied the systematic approaches in controlling operations. Compton described lower level activities in developing manufacturing line processes (1997). The actions Compton detailed systematic process logic approaches using Taylor's concepts of task time and structured management of the activities. Processes such as queuing, regression model, simulation models, and benchmarking describe Compton's approach to determining actual manufacturing operations. Compton believed in creating world class systems understand the future of system development and analyze the effect of such changes to the manufacturing environments. Compton stated integrated manufacturing systems are evidence of world-class systems, as well (1992). In some aspects, Compton aligned with Dhillon in philosophies for creating quality products. Dhillon further provided mathematical concepts to aid reliability, quality, etc engineers develop standard processes to build and deliver quality products (1996). Dhillon suggested using concurrent design methods to align production process and design specific verifications (1998). Dhillon also extended the engineering system develop process by describing methods for Value Engineering and Configuration Management. Dhillon defined value engineering as "a management technique used to perform analysis of an item function with the objective of achieving the desirable function at the minimum cost" (1998, p. 174). Dhillon additionally described the sublevel phases to value engineering. These phases are listed:

- the team selection phase
- the information collection phase
- the brainstorming phase
- the alternative evaluation phase
- the alternative development phase
- the recommendation phase
- the implementation phase (Dhillon, 1998, p. 174).

Dhillon defined configuration management as "the technical description and arrangement of items that are capable of fulfilling the fit, form, or functional needs outlined by the concerned product specification and drawings" (1998, p. 180). Dhillon focus on the design process demonstrated the high level of importance he places in creating the product. Dhillon later described general Total Quality Management systems and Program Management philosophies in continued advancements in Engineering Management (1998). These concepts exist within the system development life cycle approach used by industry in product development. In the accomplishing, this concept Compton challenged engineers to broaden their skills to understand the other functional responsibilities (1997).

Compton was clear in applying the concepts developed productivity will improve. In concert with that concept, quality will also improve (Compton, 1997). Dhillon drove engineers to be more analytical in their product development and apply scientific methods in decision-making (1998).

In dissimilarity to both Compton and Dhillon, Miller's approach excluded the details of using specific engineering design processes. Miller's application of design processes allowed members of the specified relationships implementation their independent internal processes. The major integrations aligned to the development of the risk discovered during each phase of the engineering development process.

CONCLUSION

In summary, the Engineering System Design process is a vital foundation to product development. The challenge is to management the steps in these lower level processes within system design. As established by Taylor task management fundamentally structures the engineering and production process. In all cases, Taylor's concepts underline the evolution of engineering today. Taylor's methods for manufacturing moved industrial development to the next level. The developments of Compton focused more in the area if manufacturing engineering. Compton's theories encompassed methods such as queuing and JIT processes while structuring business processes around the products. Compton exclude processes specific to designing products. Within the works of Compton, there are few references to design specifications. The attention Compton's gave to manufacturing emphasized his commitment to quality and production best practices: while Dhillon's approach aligned more to system development life cycle processes. Dhillon introduced concepts like design specifications and design reviews, as well as production concepts. Dhillon provided illustration for design optimizations and details for required functional skills. Dhillon offered systematic understanding of design phasing and structured approaches to reliability and failure analysis. Dhillon's recommended close-loop processes for quality control similar to the information Compton provides. The system development process from Miller's perspective depends greatly on what both Compton and Dhillon suggested. Miller focused on risk introduced internal to the development processes. Miller's approach encouraged engineers and business personnel to consider the complete product. Miller recommended analysis from inception to disposal and any hindrances that may occur during the life cycle of the product. Miller's focused entirely on international product development. Miller built bridges for cross corporation development.

Engineering management is specific to managing engineering products. Each theorist provided a different dimension of the process. Where Taylor developed the baseline, all other theorist expanded the process to have successful products. The theorists provided approaches that can be synthesized creating a complete life cycle approach to developing, manufacturing, and disposal of the product.

CHAPTER 2

*Engineering Management Implementations
across Industries*

The implementations of the engineering management philosophies expand many fields. For example Bhandary described the principles for the implementation of Engineering Management within the health industry. The focus on process development aids the hospital in efficiencies. Bhandary highlights that hospital management goals are similar to engineering. The need to have effective and efficient processes reflects the drive of hospital administrators to incorporate engineering management processes improving hospital care. Bhandary suggests that hospital need personnel with management skills developed by engineering management training. Having such personnel affects the hospitals in areas of cost-cutting measures and waste reduction. Bhandary states the implementation of such process were beneficial to the structured environment.

Bhandary's insight demonstrates that engineering management processes are applicable in many settings. The skills assist various areas within the environment for stream lining processes and other methods for productivity improvements. Program management is part of the engineering management process; program management specifically is not discussed specifically within this article. The management technique gives insight to individuals creating internal processes demonstrating functional relevance.

In the international markets engineering management has had an influence. Botero et al. compares the academic implementation of Engineering Management within the countries Colombia and Peru to the system in the U.S. Engineering Management began in Colombia and Peru in the early 1880s. The implementation of EM focuses around mining in the countries. Botero et al. further describes the evolution of the engineering management studies within South America. During 1959, the school's named engineering management titles were administration engineering. Many institutions renamed the universities during the 1970s. During the 1980s, the program changes and emphasizes of managing entities beyond mines move the field of study to more manufacturing industries. Both the Latin and American programs had similar structured courses. The curriculum and calendar semesters for the Latin program are longer. The strategic management processes are also similar for the Latin and American programs. The issues facing the Latin programs are the same strategic challenges affecting the American course structure, such as globalization. Each system looks to provide individuals with the soft and hard engineering skills necessary for engineering environments.

The analysis of the engineering management field described by Botero et al. contributes to the body of work developed within engineering management, yet it does little to provide implementation processes for aligning the programs of South America and America. The program does not provide statistical data for development or growth in the region of the world.

Botero et al. insight in the evolution of Engineering Management field of study in Latin America illustrates the influence globally. The data discussed reviews the present curriculum and the areas of growth. The article provides assists in aligning the American system to that of Latin America.

Engineering Management concepts were described by Componation et al performing a comparison analysis of programs within NASA. Data extracted from the NASA programs are program performance examining both team effectiveness and system engineering methodology. Componation et al begins with the review of programs selected by a constructed committee developed specifically for this process. Componation et al results state that team effectiveness for the programs selected maintained a compromising environment. The results demonstrated that most programs scored very low in the area of logical decomposition and decision analysis. The researchers surmised the issue evolved from three areas of lack within design and development. This area specifically focused was system engineering. Overall, the engineering groups worked well as a team. The findings stated individual system engineering functions contribute to the success or failure of all programs.

Componation et al provides meaningful methods for project analysis. The instruments used provide a system approach to root cause of project failures. In completing the analysis, the authors used many survey instruments to determine team function and performance. Using instruments created by Carl Larson, Frank Lafasto, Robert Blake, and Jane Mouton, the authors were able to demonstrate the team effectiveness and performance. The development of successful projects depends greatly on the engineering expertise of its members.

Componation et al demonstrates the need to have integrated processes. The full concept of engineering management is inclusive of more than design and development processes. The awareness of budget and schedule were additional parameters of success.

Additionally Jain et al. highlights the use of system development processes. These processes attribute to accelerated delivery of products. The lifecycle of the products calls for corporations to evaluate methods to improve the market share. The article compares methods to gain advantages to market. The methods reviewed were 'Modified Waterfall', 'Evolutionary Development', 'Design-to-Tool', and 'Design-to-Cost'. These were further higher-level processes applied. Each process even further diverges to more detail steps in development processes to accelerate deliveries. The article suggested metrics on these development practices further solidify feasible approaches. The article also highlighted additional methods, yet provided no recommendations on usage. Generally, the application techniques were software development processes. The application of such processes to a non-IT environment needs further research.

Specifically, Jain et al. provides methods for broaden the design process for market capture. The extension of methods and review of applications moves engineering management beyond the typical manufacturing focus.

The instrument used in the article was a comparison table listing the following attributes: Adaptability, Cost Scoping, Time Sensitivity, Evolutionary, Technology Tradeoffs, Return-on-Investment, Testing and Integration, Requirements, Risk Reduction, and Iterative Development. Additional research recommendations would add detail to the usage of these processes and the effectively.

In contrast Jones highlights the mistakes course works makes in teaching and applying program management practices to engineering projects. The 'Sunny Day Scenarios' students encounter are far from what takes place in the work environment. The article gives detail to how the development of real world problems in class makes better program managers. The article then provides method useful in creating workable engineering plans. The areas its covers are resource leveling, critical path analysis, adjustments in the critical path the meet project date and affects of optimization and risk to a program.

Jones thoughts were insightful yet he has no data for research validity. The program management applications are suggestions to assist program managers. Using Jones' work as informative in program development and program management aids student development. It is an overall aid the any engineering program.

Karimi et al. enterprise resource planning (ERP) systems implementation stated expectation from most corporations was an increase to profitability with the installation of new ERP systems. Two questions were developed to complete the review of ERP implementations to realize the expected return on investment. One question centered on the activities of the information systems (IS) organization involvement. The second question reflected the actual capabilities of the implemented ERP system. Karimi et al. structured the conversation around three areas information systems resources, the ERP resources, and the company business process. Each area provide sub levels of issues and questions, such that a full analysis required five hypothesis constructs to evaluate the proposed research questions around such implementations. To understand IS resources the article reviews of the umbrella concepts structured as the foundation of the IS. These areas associated with IS in knowledge management within the system, the relationship of this information to knowledge resources, and the actual information technology personnel. The analysis of the core functionality delivered in the ERP system pose the next level of comprehension. The functional applications available may be an asset or may not depend on the last area of analysis. This area is the internal business process. The conceptual mappings of relationships show the internal network of resources and application implementation. The results demonstrate IS resources are important factors to the successful implementation of ERP systems. The data demonstrates the success of the business process and the functionality deployment controls and directed by the IS resources. These individuals have more technical and infrastructure knowledge understanding value stream mapping of data and networking. In the implementation of such systems management should be aware of issues and communication processes between the IS resources and the process individuals. An awareness of functional relationships improves the corporate return on investments of such systems. Karimi et al. provided validity data and detail research applications suggesting methods for analysis increased awareness of the various relationships contributing to engineering management systems.

The instrument used by Karimi et al. was a survey designed to include a specific measurement system centered on the areas of information systems resources, the ERP resources, and the company business process. Additional variables added to the validity of the analysis. Customized scales aided in the collection and analysis of the relationships. Karimi et al. used a domain sampling technique in to develop the scales for validity. To aid in the validity of the data a pilot survey implementation took place using Fortune 1000 companies and later an additional survey was extracted from a known manufacturing company's housed in a national database. The pilot survey was a mail-in process. The data analysis completion took place using an ANOVA to understand the manufacturing firms and the fortune 1000 companies ERP implementations. The raw data collected from the survey input to the research model was partial least square method. In completing this process, two steps allowed the model usage to be more accurate. Karimi et al. completed measurement validation steps and manually fit data to the structured model. In the development four total models, implementations allowed the authors to build a consistent valid analysis of the data.

Kocaoglu experience in engineering management and his perspective of activities in the field describes the evolution of the last twenty years. In the early 1970s, corporations requested developing students with management skills and engineering skills. Universities answered the call creating Engineering Management programs and degrees. The article speaks of the struggle universities had in getting students. As the field of study evolved, the technology and engineering management needs continue to develop. The development of peer-reviewed journals and universities with accredited programs became driving factors to meet industry needs. Government grants and fellowship expand the depth and knowledge the practice of engineering management. Specific programs considered were University of Pittsburgh and University of Missouri Rolla. These programs seemed to provide more opportunities to individuals looking for expert education in the EM field. During the 1990s the American Society for Engineering Management started, it aided academia in identifying areas of growth needed. The author lists challenges to the development in the area as continued funding sources for research, apply the knowledge to the industry and development of green initiatives in managing these opportunities. There is important data descried in reference to the journals published, yet nothing contributing the industry application of engineering management. Kocaoglu's publishing to grow the knowledge base of engineering management. The analysis completed referrers only to the continued development of the field. No additional market data is demonstrated or communicated.

Kotnour et al. speaks to strategies developed to evolve the engineering management field of study. The biggest issues described by Kotnour et al. are the changing roles of the engineer. The history of EM developed from a need for engineers in management roles requiring business skills. Kotnour et al. reviews the history of management with the works of F. Taylor and forward. Looking at the present state of the field the MBA and traditional engineering demonstrate the career paths of managers. Given that, these skills cross many boundaries in program development. The discovery of these linkages illustrates that engineering management applies to three distinct areas. These areas are discipline-specific engineering management, general engineering management, and technology management. There are journals, societies, and educational conferences that contribute to the expansion of the field. The future structure of engineering management has issues to continue its development. The issues influence overall business development, such as organizational impacts, engineering development environment, and corporate environments. Kotnour et al. tactical questions affect the future knowledge development of these business issues. The requirements to develop educational programs, validate the knowledge gathered, and provide support to the industry in areas of need. The educational needs align to ABET and accredited programs. The knowledge gather practice requires contributes providing continued funds to support the development. The industry support requires technical and business expertise available to corporate productions and development entities. In the development of all these structure specific components must be present such as product Life cycle philosophies, process development, and technical contributions implementing the philosophies.

Kotnour et al. provides structured view of the go forward path for engineering management. The alignment of philosophies and linkages of additional fields of science demonstrate the broad reach of engineering management and its evolution over the last 90 years. It provides a view of areas requiring additional research.

Mizell et al. details the program management applications for large software programs. The approach analyzed demonstrates simulation techniques in completing estimates for the development of software. Based on the large number of software programs that generally underestimates the true cost by 25 -50 %. The software estimates traditionally use COCOMO. Mizell et al. states that this method is not applicable to all software development programs. The simulation technique suggested is the Process Analysis Tradeoff Tool (PATT) to assess the development. The use of industry standards allows individuals to understand the software size, effort, rework, as well as defect and corrections. A comparison of traditional estimation methods and the simulation technique demonstrated that the simulation method actually provides the accurate data in estimations. The simulation method provides interval data identifying KSLOC size, project length, and testing length.

Concerning engineering management, Mizell et al. expands the engineering area managed. Mizell et al. goes beyond the standard manufacturing methods described as key focal points of engineering management.

Mizell et al. provides a meaningful method for estimating software development design, including specific design steps used in program development. Mizell et al. completes the analysis by applying a side-by-side comparison of the three approaches. The analogy with simulation, analogy with cost Estimating, and bottoms-up estimate comparison provided data mathematical application in the development of hours and SLOC. The simulation process is not a typical method with the analogy, yet it demonstrated that its usefulness stem from understanding key complexities and highlighted key performance area for metric analysis.

Sauser et al. describes the growing trend in system development such that management activities expand exponentially to align to the systems. Sauser et al. suggest methods for management of programs in this space. System of System Management (SoS) process extends the single point solution to be inclusive of a large number of entities. The article defines the concept of system and its evolution. In this process the article, re inarates that traditional program management excludes additional activities required to take place. The process of SoS thinking where development of singular systems includes the layering of additional systems to extend functionality. In the management of the system, the phase used is structure chaos. This is due to the incorporating of multiple layers of design and development life cycles that occur in the development of SoS architectured items. To explain the process even more analogies to the DNA structure align to the complexity of the systems and the integrations that occur. Sauser et al. segments the systems having five qualifying functionality. Integrations and interface developments extend relationships broadening the responsibility of functional capability, where the program manager awareness and understanding is important to program success.

Sauser et al. expands the design and development practices of engineering management. The analysis of system within systems demonstrates the need to have management methods at all levels with a project or program. Sauser et al. analysis approach to system demonstrates an innovative method for system creations.

Sauser et al. provides philosophy application to the development of independent, yet integrated system. The analysis of the independent system aligns to the five areas suggested. These areas are autonomy, belonging, connectivity, diversity, and emergence. These characteristics provide a system of interconnections for developing systems. The SoS process creates method for architecture beyond individual entities.

Singer highlights specific activities and methods to avoid experiencing these program problems. Singer suggests using parallel processing, complete simulations early in the program, understand technology market development prospects, understand resources skills, understand budget constraints, and know your high priority items. These suggestions can assist for the successful completion of programs.

Singer provides engineering management personnel key concepts in the planning, executing and completion of a program. The concepts are applicable throughout the life cycle of the program. The list is inclusive of engineering skills, as well as, business skills. Singer also speaks to the soft skills of communication needed to be a good engineering program manager.

Venigalla et al, describes the application of an automated engineering management system. The system provides a collaborative environment for information sharing and discussion for a variety of engineering functions. The concept illustration focuses on a project in Virginia. The integration of the functions establishes core technical needs of the engineers. The system includes 3D modeling applications and tools. The process provides real time functional implementations of engineering solutions. Included in these tools sets are mapping capabilities for structure and architectural analysis. The label is geographical information system (GIS). The GIS is off-the-shelf software structured in a sub-component and sub-system format. The article applies the methodology to the Virginia project evaluating the sewer needs and modeling flow capacities. The tools created 3D images of the area project. The tools allowed the engineers to analyze long-term application needs and exponential environment growth. Using the GIS increase the productivity of the team and cut program cost in the development implementation of the system. The use of the system provided a 65% cost saving to the Virginia Municipality.

The systematic approach of the project contributes to engineering management in providing methods for change management within a community entity. The system data collected demonstrated methods for program improvement, which are management initiatives. Using the analysis approach for the program demonstrated engineering process application to any environment.

Venigalla et al, demonstrates a unique application of technology for engineering management purposes. The application of these tools provide flexibility and extension of skills need to implement programs intra networks.

CHAPTER 3

What Does This Mean to My Corporation?

This is a synthesized review of literature establishing engineer management philosophies implemented in the industry today and theoretical applications developed through evolution within the engineering management field of study. Including a comparison of Compton, Dhillon, Miller and Taylor's engineering management methodologies and current system process implementations, as well as contrasting engineering management concept in the development of system improvements and environmental improvements illustrating the relationships between systems around methods. Furthermore this is a comparison and contrast analysis of engineering environment and non-engineering environment implementations.

The engineering management philosophies created by these individuals define a fundamental approach to the design, development, and manufacturing of products. The foundations of their concepts provided industries with revolutionary methods for controlling the production of product, as well as complete program management philosophies for a holistic development of systems. The application of such processes provided companies with systematic approaches to meet the customer requirements (Compton, 1997). In implementation of task, management brought the high level of profit to the corporation, while paying labors at a reasonable rate (Taylor, 1967).

In reviewing implementations, today articles provided the present and historical view of engineering management. All articles reviewed are peer-reviewed articles created in the last 5 years. In many of the article, Taylor and other organizational development theorist align to the fundamental concepts. The implementation of the concepts supplied the authors with foundational structures to produce course and degree applications in building the field and body of knowledge for engineering management. Many of the articles provided realistic implementation of engineering management processes. The application of engineering management discussed in a few of the articles specifically pertains to managing engineering projects.

ENGINEERING MANAGEMENT

The Engineering Management discipline has been in existence for almost century. The beginning stages developed out of need and recognition of manufacturing process costs. The works of Taylor illustrated overall major constraints that existed in manufacturing. The issue of workers relationships and measurement systems increase cost in producing product (Taylor, 1911). The desire to pay the worker more, maintain the quality of product, and decrease time to market drove much of the work of Taylor and Gnatt. Later, Taylor included the work of Gnatt and other developing theorist on product management during the 1920s. All of these innovations resulted in the engineering management systems of today.

In building, the body of knowledge articles written by Mizell (2007), Karimi, Somers, and Bhattacherjee (2007), Componation, Youngblood, Utley, and Farrington (2008), and Jain and Chandrasekaran (2009) contain information on areas such as design process, estimations, and implementation processes for engineering projects. Areas not covered are specific business process topics or general manufacturing. Whiles others provide time-line pictures of engineering management and it beginnings, as well as steps to create a future for engineering management. Little data from these articles demonstrated areas of application. In any case, the overall approach to the field of study and general implementations demonstrated there are many additional methods and concepts to discuss in additional articles not presented here.

Engineering management past. The academic structures of engineering management developed to support industrial practices based on corporate needs. Engineering management in a broad since expands many disciplines. For the extraction of a central definition, one would include core engineering, manufacturing concepts and a few business methodologies. The structured system of engineer management continued to reach beyond the general bodies of product production. Articles written by Omurtag (2009), Kotnour and Farr (2005), Botero and Castro (2005), and Kocaoglu (2009) examine the history and the future of the field engineering management, while all other reviewed articles were application focused.

Engineering management philosophies find roots in the development of engineering administration in 1914 (Omurtag, 2009). Similarly, Kotnour et al documented the first degrees created in the field focused in industrial engineering in 1909 at Massachusetts Institutes of Technology (2005). Kotnour et al also highlighted the fact that engineering administration evolved after World War II (2005). Using many of the methods of Taylor, we discover the fundamental applications. Taylor's concept structured an approach to manufacturing products based on specific job task. The course developed at MIT in 1914 focused on developing men to manage business where engineering issues took place (Omurtag, 2009). This was shortly after the release of Taylor's writing in 1911. The course defined many of the central skills Taylor highlights, as necessary talents, managers should have (Taylor, 1911).

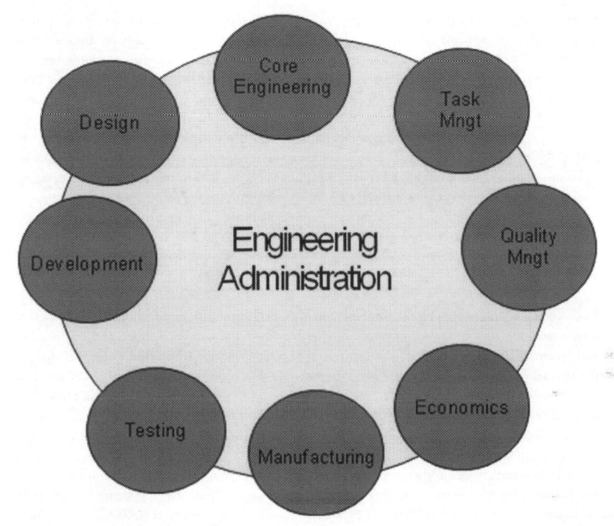

Figure 1. Engineer Management Past

As concepts like quality management and statistical process, development began to take root in building stable manufacturing processes, the requirement to manage issues discovered within these environments advanced management's and engineer's involvement. This growth took place between the 1940s and 1960s (Kotnour et al, 2005). In parallel portions of South America began embracing academic needs to create specific environments for the development of engineers for management within the National Faculty of Mines (Botero et al., 2005). The National Faculty of Mines was initially a National University under the control of Colombia and Peru's national government (Botero et al., 2005). This development demonstrates the wide reaching needs of engineering administration expertise and its global impact (Botero et al., 2005). In contrast to American academics, the South American programs focused its engineering population in the areas of civil and mining engineering core applications (Botero et al., 2005). The bridged concepts of business and industrial management introductions began in the 1950s (Botero et al., 2005). During the 1960s, the field of engineering evolved introducing a growing need for electrical, mechanical, and civil etc, as well as the science specifically in America began to structure itself around industrial engineering focusing on aspects of manufacturing (Omurtag, 2009). Academia continued to evolve with this need, as stated by both Omurtag and Kocaoglu. Within this time of history, the degree programs developed across the globe. The decision to change the discipline name came with many discussions (Kocaoglu, 2009). An agreement on the name change from administration to management officially took place 1980s (Kocaoglu, 2009). The primary area of development for the discipline's creation, solidifying the name demonstrated the level of skills required in being an engineering manager (Kocaoglu, 2009). The interesting discovery was the fundamental definition of engineering management remained undetermined (Kocaoglu, 2009). Rather the course foundation structured and curriculum details described areas such as decisions making, industrial engineering, and quality engineering management. In describing these course aspects of a holistic system application, appeared to provide the foundation. The courses are technical, financial, organizational, business marketing and production processing (Omurtag, 2009). In many of Dhillon and Compton's writing philosophical applications of statistical practices created by both Deming and Shewart defined quality implementations and similar process are part of product analysis for design and development. Compton and Dhillon specifically embraced the task management processes Taylor created. These processes documented in the 1911 paper of Taylor became the fundamentally details of courses provided by MIT in 1914.

Engineering management present. The evolution of the field seemed to stager behind the development of new technologies. Industrial engineering core remained the baselined aspects of engineering management. In the comparison, the definitions of both Compton and Dhillon are inclusive of specific task aligned to the skill areas defined in more business course work. With continued changes in the market during the early eighties, needs and product evolutions required new organizations for engineer expertise and engineering management. The introduction of Dhillon, Hicks, and Compton's work advanced engineering management in the corporate industry, while university system began adding core program management skills to curriculums in later years. Many programs began to expand to master degrees in the field, as well as Ph.D. level degree, increasing in the areas of study attempting to meet the new technology age for the edification of new students going into the field of engineering. The organizational and psychological areas in corporate environments brought a level of soft skills required for the engineering industries. The core engineering design processes and application became a spoke in the wheel of the body of knowledge. The core engineering skills demonstrate the hard areas of knowledge in development of product. During this time, many fields became a part of the philosophies of engineering management.

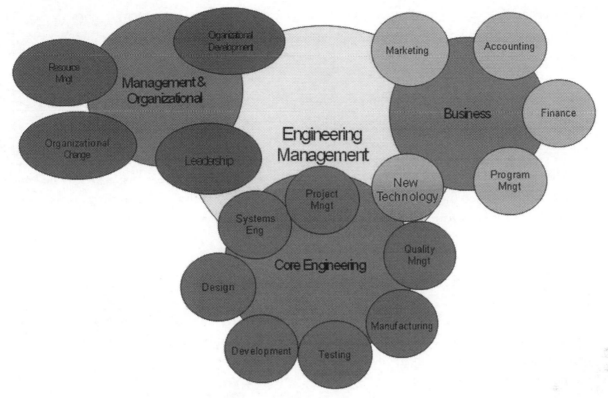

Figure 2. Engineering Management Present

In many of these cases, engineering management definitions began to evolve.

Table 2.

Definitions of Engineering Management (Kotnour et al, 2005, p.17)

Definition	Reference
Engineering management is designing, operating, and continuously improving purposeful systems of people machines, money, time, information, and energy by integrating engineering and management knowledge, techniques, and skills to achieve desired goals in technological enterprise through concern for the environment, quality, and ethics.	Omurtag (1988)
The engineering manager is distinguished from other managers because he or she possesses both the ability to apply engineering principles and a skill on organizing and directing people and projects. He or she is uniquely qualified for two types of jobs: the management of technical functions (such as design or production) in almost any enterprise; or the management of broader functions (such as marketing or top management) in a high technology enterprise.	Babcock and Morse (2002)

Engineering management is the discipline addressed to making and implementing decisions for strategic and operational leadership in current and emerging technologies and their impacts on interrelated systems.	IEEE (1990) and Kocaoglu (1991)
Engineering management is the art and science of planning, organizing, allocating resources, and directing and controlling activities that have a technological component.	American Society for Engineering Management

In reviewing these definitions, most align to theorist illustrated the expansion of engineering management described by Taylor during the 1900s. The need to include organizational areas, and business processes demonstrated the inclusive nature of engineering management.

Table 3.
KAM VI Theorist Definition of Engineering Management

Definition	Reference
Engineering management is concerned with managing engineering and technologies to achieve business objectives, and it requires skills in understanding technology and engineering in addition to managing business activities of organizations.	Dhillon (2002, p. 33)
The role of management is to lead and create an organization and an atmosphere that can fulfill its goals and missions.	Compton (1997, p. 108)
The principal object of management should be to secure the maximum prosperity for the employer, coupled with the maximum prosperity for the employee.	Taylor (1967, p. 9)
The program management is the management of risk. There are two types of risk to manage. The decisioneering risk and managerial approaches, where decisioneering is general management decision evaluating profit and return on investment based on specific actions. The managerial approach is the development of strategic methods to avoiding system technical risk.	Miller (2000, p 85)
Engineering Management is the organizing, planning, staffing, directing, leading, and controlling of the activities of engineers, scientists, designer, draftsmen, and other technical and nontechnical personnel, to achieve desired goals in the design, manufacturing, construction, operation, or maintenance of a product, device, structure, or machine.	Hick (1966, p.4)

> Engineering management is different from functional management   Shannon (1980, p 13)
> in the following ways: technical management requires a certain
> amount of flexibility based on technical applications and innovation:
> technical management estimation are structured differently based
> on analysis of new technologies: with new technologies technical
> managers development cost structures with no historical data: technical
> manager must understand market share production and product life
> cycle implementations: technical managers have to understand task
> performance in the development process

The perspectives exemplify the broad approach to engineering management and the technology inputs. As stated in many definitions engineering core activities are key areas of management. Interestingly enough theorist definitions specifically address the function of engineering management while Babcock et al. focused on the individual activities. Fundamentally, all depicted engineering management as activities centered around management of resources etc. on engineer programs. All contain emphasized of business related concepts i.e. market share and strategic goals. The approach to relating these topics to areas of business demonstrated the link between product development and market share for product distribution (Compton, 1997). Omurtag said little in the development of business opportunities, yet stated, "continuously improving purposeful systems of people machines, money, time, information, and energy" (Kotnour et al. 2005, p. 17) which related to that area of business development.

In developing, the overall system of engineering management Kotnour et al. demonstrated the overarching areas the field of study covers. Kotnour et al. segments engineering management into five specific disciplines. In concert with the definitions, provided Kotnour et al. list the following:

- Engineering disciplines
- Discipline-specific engineering management
- Generalist engineering management
- Management of technology
- General Management (Kotnour et al., 2005, p. 17).

Kotnour et al. summarized these areas into "(a) discipline-specific engineering management, (b) generalist engineering management, and (c) management of technology "(2005, p. 17) highlighting the cross functional application of industrial engineering. Most of these areas exclude specific business related elements of studies. The application of program management skills are also excluded yet within the definitions such attributes are highlighted by Kotnour et al. Such additional layering in the knowledge base is demonstrated in Dhillon definition.

In the expanding of engineering management, the focus on development cost and manufacturing practiced extends the concept of management to include design methodologies, final product, and product life cycle management (Dhillon, 2002). In many cases, Dhillon provided additional strategies to create solid philosophies and methodologies for implementing an engineering program. Where Compton focused in the task management portion of program management, Kotnour et al. (2005) determined this to be an important area of focus for the future in developing engineering's manager.

Kotnour et al. (2005) specifically highlights such areas based on globalization and need to implement program management processes virtually and bi-coastally. As technologies, evolve for many types of product development the need to manage these items progress also. In the writings of Kotnour et al. (2005), issues and boundary challenges are the objective of his communication, as well as Kocaoglu. Kotnour et al. described themes and constructs he determined halts the development of engineering management as a skilled area for expansion (2005). Issues such as research funding, a more service structured market rather than manufacturing, and emerging new technologies are areas Kocaoglu described as boundaries (2009). The umbrella nature of engineering management seemed to drive the science to implementing and training necessary soft skills for leadership and organizational impacts (Kotnour et al, 2005). The hard skills draw deeply on the mathematical backgrounds of engineers with core skill training (Kotnour et al, 2005). In many cases the concepts of engineering management has not out lived the rumored reasoning in 1960s for its creation. Engineering management program labels were "In addition there was a need to create a softer, alternative path for students enrolling in the classical engineering discipline who were findings them to be unmanageably demanding. (Omurtag, 2009, p. 4)" Omurtag even stated,

> In the early days, the program at Rolla was a "salvage operation". That is, it was set up partly to catch the drop-outs from the classical engineering disciplines. At that time UM-Rolla was very technical in nature, and there were very few alternatives on campus for a student who had difficulty with math and sciences; however, the university wanted to keep them on campus. (2009, p. 33)

Illustrating the lack of understanding in alignment to the practice demonstrated within industry. Kotnour et al. further defined trends that influence the additional layering of engineering management (2005).

Table 4.
Trends in Engineering Management (Kotnour et al., 2005)

Discipline	Soft	Hard/Soft	Hard
Organizational	Forging partnerships		
	Operating networks of relationships		
	Gaining/maintaining employee loyalty and commitment		
	Managing and leading teams		
	Managing and leading workforces		
	Changing culture		

	The needed management and leadership skills and behaviors		
Technical		Implementing a process-based organization	
		Continuously managing change	
			Using tools and metrics to manage
Business		Understanding and managing uncertainty	

Each of these areas demonstrated the additional skills in organizational management deemed necessary for the field of study. Further, Kotnour et al. provided points of strategic implementation to counter act concepts deemed challenges to developing engineering management and engineering managers. These strategies are as follows:

- Certification of Engineering Management Programs
- Engineering Management Research Agenda
- Engineering Management Technical Assistance Agenda
- Certification of the Engineering Management Professional
- Integration of Engineering Management Knowledge Roles
- Body of Knowledge
- Integration of Engineering Management Professional Societies (Kotnour et al., 2009, pp. 23-25).

These items emphasized the need to train, to expand the knowledge base, and to build the body of knowledge around engineering management. Within the field of engineer science evolution are continuous and as such, the arena to study, grow knowledge professionally, and apply knowledge evolved.

Many articles highlighted the upcoming impact of globalization on engineering management. The impact basis determined in manufacturing and new technology development taking place around the globe force creators within the field to comprehensively expand engineering management. The ultimate purpose was to meet the growing need for engineering individuals with business development skills capturing a foot hold on new markets around the globe. The institutions in South America see a great need to expand their curriculum to the application of law and detail courses in business marketing (Botero et al., 2005). Additional areas of concern are rapid turnaround for profit, the diversity of staff, and standardizations of process for interactions with environments and communities. Dhillon, Taylor, and Compton all suggested that most management is engineering trained individuals.

In the evolution of engineering definitions to system development and product life cycles, the inclusion of practical business approaches pointed out the need for Master's degrees in business. Very few core-engineering curriculums have any emphasized on business philosophies of market analysis and profit analysis during the early 1980s (Kotnour et al., 2005). Componation (2008) suggested, as well as Kotnour et al. (2005) business application of product, industry, and environmental analyses are improvements to the field of study. Kotnour et al. (2005) identified knowledge areas of engineering management. These knowledge areas highlighted the board impact of engineering management. The concept of life cycle, system program management, organizational methods, and financing along with additional business processes demonstrated the inclusive needs of engineering management. The processes of management within these areas highly align to themes introduced by Dhillon and Compton. Dhillon required analytical analysis of data for corporate consideration (2002). Dhillon's focus on profit analysis and costing structures illustrated the expansion of the roles the engineer's possess (1989). As listed in Dhillon's ideas of engineering's task environmental awareness are key to new business development.

Engineering management progressed to new levels on the basis on technology. With the continued development of new science, methods, and products, technology drives the need for engineering managers. The understanding of environmental factors and cost structures demonstrated the success and/or failure of many corporations. Engineering training produced systematic thinking skills applicative to various business structures.

ENGINEERING MANAGEMENT PROCESSES

The development of engineering skills aligned to analytical processing and decision analysis concepts. In the creation of product, major areas to consider are the design and development of the product. Within engineering management's body of knowledge, organizational processes, system development processes, and business processes contributed to the foundation. To apply the system of engineering management some articles focused on the development stages/phases of the process. The system development life cycle contributed to the structured definition of engineering management, as well as business development models. Kotnour et al. (2005) exposed the business skills requirements in the engineering management definitions table 1 above. As part of this review, articles applied the actual engineering skills to manage programs are included. Engineering management focused in the managing of engineering project and programs, yet there are specific aspects of business to consider. Business market analysis demonstrated an area included in engineering decisions. According to Dhillon (1987), these processes are lower level driver to the manufacturing lines, product sales, and obsolescence reviews. These processes revealed the linkages between the philosophies of business development, engineering innovation for market share, organizational development, and organizational learning.

ORGANIZATIONAL AND SYSTEM DESIGN APPLICATIONS.

Organizational applications. In review of the philosophical approaches to engineering management, organizational structures and hierarchies can influence program development. Dhillon introduced organizational functions and program matrix approaches to managing engineering programs (1987). In the creation of the organization, the team's attributes under consideration are effectiveness, efficiencies, and productivity. Componation et al. (2008) completed research designed to evaluate correlations between subcomponent concepts of engineering management such as system engineering, team effectivity, and project management themes (2008). Componation et al. defined methods for implementing system engineering within engineering management constructs (2008). Componation et al. results emphasized the relationships presence between organization, technical decision making i.e. system engineering implementations, and program management (2008). Comparatively these processes are fundamentally the approaches described by both Dhillon and Compton. The structured presence of the team Componation et al. described aligns to a scoring scale of effectivity (2008). Componation et al. instrument used for the analysis evolved from the work of Robert Blake and Jane Mouton (2008). The scale described the teams functioning in the following ways:

- Push for Production
- Country Club
- Improvised
- Compromise
- Teamwork (Componation et al., 2008, pp. 41-42).

These descriptions summarize many years of collective research on teams and groups. Each term described how the manager or management interacted with the team (Componation et al., 2008). It also described the management style of the manager in the execution of tasks (Componation et al., 2008). These concepts fundamentally aligned to both Compton and Dhillon. Both Compton and Dhillon described in detail what the organizational core should contain and actual skills required for the organization members. In each case, Dhillon and Compton highlighted the skills of both engineers as engineers and engineers as managers. In the process of implementation, Karimi et al. identified the need to have structured organization (2007). Karimi et al. recognized the impact of resource availability and skill level specifically when delivering new capabilities to technical systems (2007). Karimi's et.al research focused on implementation failures of an enterprise resource-planning systems (2007). Karimi's et al. results demonstrated that in particular information system resources are important to the distribution of enterprise resources planning systems (2007). The study demonstrated the relationships that exist between top-level management, functional resources, and information system resources (Karimi's et al., 2007). The overall impact on the organization identified two specific areas for successful implementation (Karimi's et al., 2007). The importance of top-level management needed to demonstrate to the organization the strategic necessity of implementing the system (Karimi's et al., 2007). The functional resource identified the required capabilities for the organization, while the information system resource builds the information technology portion of the project (Karimi's et al., 2007). In any event, the management and communication of such systems is the responsibility of an engineering manager (Dhillon, 2002). The organizational influences are important to the success of program implementation (Dhillon, 2002).

System development applications. In the development of engineering management, core-engineering skills contributed foundationally to manager's ability to manage (Dhillon, 2002). Understanding the design process of system development described in Kotnour et al. (2005), Omurtg (2009), and Botero et al. (2005) writings illustrated specific training required in engineering management. Core-engineering elements defined the process of system development (Jain et al., 2009). As well as, system product life cycle elements defined curriculum course integrated into the engineering management field of study.

In concert to the concepts, Jain et al. evaluated using various design methodologies with the context of engineering management (2009). Jain et al. used system development processes to illustrate the advantages created by rapid turnaround (2009). Jain et al. proposed the use of rapid system development for agile response to market trends (2009). While Componation's et al. (2008) work described need to understand team effectiveness. Componation et al. (2008) states cohesion proved to be the foundation in having successful projects. Both Jain et al., Componation et al. evaluated the development of technical solutions based on data collected based on the projects examined (2008).

Componation et al. reviewed design processes such as requirements definition and the segmentation of these requirements (2008). The breakdown of requirements makes up system engineering implementation processes. Componation et al. further gathered criteria from an executive board to define overall program success (2008). Within this criterion, such items focused on are achieving requirements, performance to schedule, and budget management. Componation's et al. (2008) results found most programs analyzed performed well in meeting technical requirement objects, yet the process used for technical decision-making was low in scoring. The failures seemed to align to requirement logic decomposition. The teams seemed to have difficulty within the conversion of the product. The conversion of requirements to product can be difficulty based on available technology and technical skill of the team. Jain et al. provides analytical methods to create test worthy product for technical teams (2009). The methods Jain et al. described:

- Modified Waterfall (subsystem with overlapping phases)
- Modified Waterfall (Risk reduction)
- Evolutionary Prototyping
- Staged delivery/Incremental Implementation
- Feature Driven development
- Design to schedule
- Design to tools
- Design to cost (Jain et al, 2009, p. 34).

,where in each case the standard life cycle and system engineering processes illustrated the usefulness. Jain et al. proposed matrix could assist Componation et al. with areas of technical skills recognition for successful programs (2008).

The application of Jain's approach could also benefit the research completed by many other articles provided in this analysis. Although Componation's et al. finding suggested most engineering teams tend to function effectively on various programs the lower score in system decomposition suggested methods used in system development were incomplete (2008). The methods listed above are detailed design approaches that can be acclimated more to the process of requirement decomposition and development. The procedure for control at each stage emphasized the desired outputs importance to product success. In many cases, the levels of completeness for requirements dictated product functional success.

Similarly, Sauser & Boardman (2008) focused on the development of systems within systems contributing to the construct of system engineering. System engineering processes generally applied to individual systems forming a layered approach to systems within systems. Sauser et al. (2008) demonstrated the layer of systems that interact and integrate for full system functionality based on specific attributes. Sauser et al. (2008) provided an analytical structure to determine the hierarchal layer of systems. This analytical architecture structure definition existed in autonomy, belonging, connectivity, diversity, and emergence (Sauser et al., 2008). Sauser et al. stated, "We are posting that the five characteristics we have presented are elements of the architecture of a 'systems DNA'. We believe there are interlocking as they extend from one extremity to the other for each (i.e. paradox)" (Sauser et al., 2008, p. 6). Moving to system analysis in this fashion demonstrates lower level connectivity that may affect overall system functionality. The alignment of Sauser et al. (2008) to Jain's et al. (2009) rapid system development provided an integrated framework for usage of all methodologies suggested. This process was significantly different in its approach to program development stated in the reviewed articles. The system of system considerations aligned only Dhillon in the specifics of types of program. Dhillon alludes to such concepts in the development of aircraft programs (1989). The integration of systems and linkages required to produce a fully capable system underlines these philosophies.

Mizell and Malone contributed research demonstrates the simulation process of system development, using a modeling technique similar to Jain's et al. (2009) modified waterfall with risk reduction takes advantage of determining key parameters confidence levels for development. Venigalla and Baik (2007) used simulation-modeling methods to determine the data needs in the evaluation of geographic information system (GIS) tools. The system development process required a systematic approach to analyze the variety of data input and outputs required implement a complete system (Venigalla et al., 2007). The modeling techniques developed into a design by structuring the system requirements for selecting a platform (Venigalla et al., 2007). To demonstrate the broad applicability of engineering management Bhandary discussed using engineering management processes in hospital management. Bhandary determined that engineering management goals align to hospital process implementations (2007). Specific areas of consideration are process development, system efficiencies, system controls, and productivity (Bhandary, 2007).

Very few of the additional articles addressed intra engineering management processes, where system management was applicable. Componation et al. (2008), Jain et al. (2009), and Sauser et al. (2008) focused attention on system design although research demonstrates that many underlining sectors of engineering management contribute to a management success.

Program management applications. Dhillon proposed Taylor's approach to task timing and job design to produce the management of engineering (Dhillon, 1987). Similarly, many of the reviewed articles aligned in philosophy with the beginning stages of engineering management in reference to that of program or project management. Yet, only Singer and Jones provided suggestions in how to apply the engineering management skills. Singer gave specific detail actions to take on running a program (Singer, 2009). The actions Singer suggested are the following:

- Define task with parallel state dates
- Simulation of design and early testing
- Reuse of and apply new technologies
- Understand staffing and interfaces

- Understand the work in progress for identified task
- Define constraints upon finical resources
- Organizational communication

These go beyond addressing engineering design issues and defects that may occur in the manufacturing process (2009). Singer included conceptual practice of organization development and system design and development processes (2009). Singer developed his conclusion around personal experiences. Singer did not execute any detail research to support his experiences. Jones' approach focused on using program management tools and methods for resource allocation to complete engineering projects (2008). Jones revealed little information on core engineering processes (2008). Jones' application focused on critical path and optimization of task within the critical path (2008). Within both applications, engineer system development processes and understanding the organization are important to the implementation. As did Singer, Jones provided no supporting data justifying his experience. The information provided is the personal experience of Jones. Jones suggested these methods as best practice for any company. In comparison to Dhillon, Jones highlighted the need to understand program management, as well as cost in developing and selecting projects (Dhillon, 2002). However, Dhillon provided an algorithmic approach to program management. Dhillon suggested using concepts like benefit-cost ratio model to determine whether projects are worth cost invested (2002). Dhillon suggested using net present value data, profitability indexes, time-to-money analysis, and risk calculations in making these decisions (2002). Dhillon suggested the roles required to complete the engineering and general task complete by them. Some of these tasks below:

- Design product
- Optimize the design
- Coordinate the design activity with all concerned individuals
- Participate in design reviews
- Produce new ideas for designs
- Keep abreast of the changing environments and technology
- Keep the design within given constraints
- Record all changes
- Keep management up to data with the design activity
- Answer design-related questions (Dhillon, 2002, p. 118).

These tasks suggested the process for planning the design and development of the project (Dhillon, 2002). Singer aligned to the above list in optimization of design by having parallel task. Singer called out the use and reuse of technology which is not possible unless the engineer abreast of the technologies and his environment. In addition to that, Singer stated to define constraints while Dhillon stated that the engineer must design within those constraints. Singer highlighted organizational communication, where Dhillon identified methods for communication such as design reviews, record of changes, keeping management in the loop of communication, and answering design questions.

As part of management process estimation of cost are components to completing a program successfully, as stated by Componation et al (2008). The process of developing estimated may include many phases of the program. In review of present applications of the process Mizell's et al. approach to software programs aligned to analytical system provided by Dhillon. Even Kotnour recognized program management and project mange with quantitative method application are component to the sub-levels of engineering management. In the process of application, Mizell's et al. analysis focused on program management processes of an engineering management. This focus revealed a combined system design process and business process. Mizell's et al. (2007) discussion highlighted the need to structure more accurate cost estimates of large software development programs. In the process of the estimate considerations of design methods align to those described by Jain required additional analytical analysis. Mizell et al. compared three approaches to creating cost estimates for large software programs (2007). Mizell et al. suggested using statistical simulation model using a discrete event process simulation (2007). This method allowed the developer to functionally walkthrough the activation of each step in the process. The process allowed the developer to determine specific areas of focus. The resulting data provided a confidence levels for various key areas in application development. The area such as lines of code, test, and verification needs, and approximation of defects introduced (Mizell et al., 2007). The model even provided estimates of years necessary for application/product completion. As discussed in the works of Jain et al. the engineering management component of this process is inclusive of all Mizell's et al. proscribed steps (2007). As well, Venigalla et al. suggested the improvement to engineer managers takes place in managing program internal to municipal governments by using the platforms designed and analyzed (2007).

In the works of Karimi et al., the research covered program management needs in analyzing the implementation of information technology program's affect the core business. The research evaluated the impact to functioning programs and planned programs by developing additional capabilities when necessary. Karimi et al. (2007) suggested that implementation process might have optimal seasons for strategic evolutions. The program manager aspects reflected on those strategies concerning resources applicable and available for the task (Karimi et al., 2007). The management of the program determines estimations of cost from the creation to obsolescence of a product. The use of engineering management skills rather than general management roles demonstrated the requirement of technical capabilities to understand the accuracy of the estimates.

The specific components of engineering management from system design and development to obsolescence processes exposed the expanding boundaries of the field. Application of engineering management within many entities in the development of systems supplied the engineering manager with information contributing to the lesson learned gathered by both Jones and Singer in program management techniques. Completing processes such as cost estimates and system design analysis drives, the manager understood the market environment and customer needs.

Business Applications

On the basis, engineering management includes finical analysis, customer needs, and cost reductions for increased profits, the next article reviews illustrate business approaches to system development. In reviewing the work of Distefano & O'Brien, customer satisfaction is a high priority. Distefano et al. research analyzed the use of three different methods for infrastructure assessments (2009). Government agencies are the prime customers for the tool. In recent year, satellite technology and palm held devices created opportunity to advance the government agency's system. The market analysis demonstrated the generational users of such items like cell phones desired similar systems for soldiers. Distefano et al. assisted in determining the usefulness of the new tools (2009). Distenfano et al. research determined that soldier preferred the handheld device with electronic interfaces (2009). In the final analysis, the recommendation was to use only the electronic system regardless of the impact to compact dress. The development of the HAMMER and GATER illustrated growth based on technology. Each are "handheld digital devices which integrates a personal digital assistant (PDA), a global positioning system (GPS) receiver, a laser range finder, a digital compass, and a digital camera" (Distenfano et al., 2009,p. 98). These items replaced the pencil and pad checklist the soldiers used before (Distenfano et al., 2009). This is an example of seeing and meeting market need based on new technology. These same tools can be useful to other organizations in urban development, as well as transportation system agencies.

Similarly, Venigalla et al. (2007) introduced systems useful in mapping and geographic analysis. Venigalla's et al. (2007) research created systems that municipal government agencies can use in the development of infrastructure of these areas. The tool suggested included core engineering function of civil engineers, such that assist in the analysis of present infrastructures and growth opportunities for that community (Venigalla's et al., 2007). The technology expansions provided by the geographic information system (GIS) included modeling and simulations for design and development (Venigalla's et al., 2007). The GIS system provided watershed data, drainage data, and runoff hydrographs (Venigalla's et al., 2007). The impact of usage for the GIS tools contributed to city and state governmental savings by aiding in developing, maintaining, and destroying infrastructure areas that are not needed (Venigalla's et al., 2007). The finical benefits to using the new technology require manager's awareness of the return on investment. Of course, the cost associated with the use of the tools must be monitored, yet the central driver to accruing the systems lay in the simulation and model techniques available for infrastructure design and development (Venigalla's et al., 2007).

In further analysis, Karimi et al. introduced research that affects the bottom-line of most manufacturing companies. The delivery of the new system provides the company with various levels of valued engineering (Karimi et al., 2007). While both Venigalla et al and Distenfano et al. examined new technologies and their impacts on customers, the evaluations of integrated platforms demonstrated business aspects of engineering management. Bhandary review included similar analysis of cost benefits. Bhandry's approach was the implementation of engineering processes within the hospital environment would improve cost. The process of selecting engineering tools to improve hospital decisions, efficiencies, and productivity, ultimately affect the core structure of the business. The analyses of new technologies are imperatives to the development of the core business.

CONCLUSION

Engineering management continued to present itself as a field that is inclusive of many disciplines. Much of this is based on the concepts of Product Life Cycles. New philosophies introduced into core-engineering fields included managing products from idea conception to disposal. Kotnour's et al discussion on the future and broadening perspective of engineering management beyond areas of just manufacturing, illustrated theories communicated by both Dhillon and Compton. The risk components introduced by Miller contribute the program management activities of the engineering manager. Risk assessments contributed to specific key parameters required for success of the project. Product lifes within any corporate environment evolve through specific stages where data from market impacts and profits returns drive the expansion. The responsibilities of management expand for knowledgeable decisions are required for product development and product evolution.

These articles illustrated three main areas of focus. Each contributed to developing the body of knowledge within engineering management. These areas include core-engineering skills, program management skills, and equipping the future with engineering management skills. Further analysis on business innovation skills mentioned at low levels in two articles demonstrates additional research areas. Engineering management's evolution came during a time when technologies expand. The landscape of engineering management continues to evolve based on the business needs of the globe.

CHAPTER 4

Methods and Implementation

Through the works of Compton, Dhillon, Miller, and Taylor we reviewed method and theories of engineering administration, known today as engineering management. These theorists provided the fundamental implementation strategies for developing successful engineering management processes. Through contemporary analysis, many of the theorist teachings remain the foundation of engineering management systems executed today. Chapter 4 will include a comparison of strategic models for developing engineering management systems and an evaluation of the success and failures of these strategic models, as well as provide a model that aligns with contemporary concepts of system implementation driven by Product Development Life Cycles. The PDLC alignments demonstrated areas of expansion in the field of engineering management and product lifecycles.

This chapter focuses on the implementations of engineering management in relationship to other disciplines that affect strategic development of products beyond manufacturing and production. It will introduce a systematic approach aligned to system lifecycles for new product development and product derivatives. The strategic implementations assist in recognizing return on investment in products and methods for product growth based on either a commercial or governmental environment. The strategies assist in implementation of product development systems based on contemporary system design methodology, emphasizing a holistic approach to complete product life cycle management. The compartmentalization of hard and soft factor terms used drives the implementations and communicates structured needs of the organization and customer. In the alignment to System Development Life Cycle, hard factors cross-domains and disciplines in usage.

Organizational change models are key contributors to creating environments open to evolutionary product development. In a border sense there may be a need to re-structure the entire organization to create product derivatives real-time. These organizational changes are driven by management decisions on product development for market share. Organizational impacts shall be highlighted in the event there is an effect on the product. Recommendations for organizational execution information provide procedural instruction to aid in the organizational evaluation.

BACKGROUND

Engineering management is an inclusive field of study. No one theorist has established a method of approach deemed centrally imperative. The areas of engineering management evolve as the technology expands its reach around the globe. Engineering management embraces the use of business skills, as well as engineering skills. The use of both concepts demonstrated applications of talented managers. Methods introduced in recent years for organizational development and organizational learning are sub-level knowledge areas. Fundamentally sound organizations with sound engineering techniques and business knowledge are examples of successful implementations.

Task management was developed for production control within the work of Fredrick Taylor. Many recognized Taylor's work as a system that focused tasks and divided planning from the manual process (Waring, 1991). Extracting from the work of Taylor, both Compton and Dhillon recognized the success companies had in implementing such strategies. Compton further recognized technology changes required new methods of management. Specifically in the area of manufacturing Compton embraced new methods in the process of production. The new methods included the use of high tech machinery and less manual involvement in actual production.   Along with this development came the introduction of program management tools. Dhillon proceed to demonstrate the need and the use of program management within manufacturing. Dhillon extends engineering management by including product life cycle costing from design to disposal. Dhillon provided a full picture of engineering management from the development of the organization and management personnel to structured management processes for selecting designs and products based strictly on the return on investment data. Miller moves design and development of engineering management to an even higher level by integrating beyond functional activities. Miller called engineering management process to integrate between entities and build partnerships.

The history of engineering management began as the industrial age began. The need to cut productions cost and control the work force inspired Taylor to create 'Scientific Management'. The fundamentally purpose for task management was to reduce production time. The definition of task management required the engineers or management of the faculty to time the Artisans in completing the creation of a product. The engineering would then segregate those times and teach the skills to different individual. Taylor's approach removed the monopoly for the artisan worker. Management managed the production at each stage in the process evaluating the time to completion for the next step. Waring stated;

> Building bureaucracy transferred the reins of power from subordinates to superiors.
> Mechanizing and specializing jobs restricted the discretion of those on the bottom of
> the organization and expanded the power of those on top. Both changes also reduced
> the cost of wages and training, since using semi-skilled workers minimized the cost
> of turnover even without lowering its rates. (Waring, 1991, p. 11)

Waring highlighted the applications of Taylor's approach were marginalized by individuals in business (1991). Waring stated the concepts of bureaucracy were deemed more useful (1991). Many believed the power distribution should not go to engineers and the administrative cost for time analysis, yet many corporations implemented the processes and experienced the immediate cost savings and reduced time to market (Waring, 1991).

In developing systems of management, identifying the tasks is a sub-level process for program management. According to Dhillon using a program evaluation and review technique assists in developing practical plan for executing to completeness on a project. Dhillon demonstrated this process in detailing program management. Dhillon provided insight to creating engineering organizations and designing technical environments with engineers as managers. Dhillon provided a view of engineering management by developing costing processes for projects. Dhillon's work is geared as fundamental philosophies in developing technical products.

Additionally Compton's approach to engineering management brought manufacturing processes into the cycle. Compton focused on the management of these activities and the integration of the technologies in manufacturing areas. Compton limited his view of system design and development. Even in the area of cost Compton used the cost structures of manufacturing and logistics. Compton fundamentally believed in developing world class manufacturing systems.

The technical industry evolves globally expanding the requirement to have engineering managers. The global impact of technology requires corporate environments and organizational to function beyond the standard design and build processes that generally exist. This process contributes to the life cycle of products. Many corporations are finding it difficult to maintain and gain market share due to the aggressively evolving technical impacts. The strategic process for companies to keep their positions lay in their ability to move product design and development to the market before a competitor. Engineering management is a central contributor to this process. The philosophies introduced by both Compton and Dhillon can be considered the foundation of such processes.

On many occasions a single company could not structure itself to handle an entire market. Due to the expansion of general market many companies have developed corporate partnerships. These partnerships align to the philosophies Miller introduced in developing risk management processes to management the programs (2000). Miller established additional methods of engineering management at high-levels based on the corporation's position in the overall program or project (2000). Miller's approach to corporate partnerships required a level of management in the area of risk (2000). Miller's suggestion of risk management illustrated the process of entities creating far reaching relationships based on engineering management philosophies (2000).

Each contributed to the development of engineering management. Full system development requires meaningful analysis to maintain cutting edge development processes and market share. This application describes product's life cycle cost and product process to complete necessary analysis at stages of the corporation and the organization.

PRODUCT LIFE CYCLE COST AND TIME TO MARKET

Domination of markets and beyond believable profit margin is drivers for corporate boardrooms to worry. Knowing your competitors and providing various products for customers drive goals and objective development. Moving the organization to high levels of productivity and efficiencies, lower production cost, and maintaining high positions in market provides a birthing ground for excellent engineering managers. The requirement to establish products with long life cycles and control markets influence corporations to develop engineering managers. Engineering managers, today, brought many additional skills to bear. The competitive view and technical knowledge engineering managers value exceeds the generally manager. The evolution of organizations, groups, and teams to embrace these concepts of a global market and expanding customer base builds the importance of engineering managers.

STRATEGIC MODEL IMPLEMENTATIONS

The emphasis in many cases of engineering management is project and product control. Control in terms of meeting cost, schedule, and quality expectations in the creation of the product. Dhillon describes program management techniques, organization development and design process implementations (2002). Dhillon suggested many lifecycle cost models illustrating the variety of products and the cost involved with these products (1989). Dhillon suggested using structured lifecycle cost analysis in determining product profits (1989). Dhillon philosophy follows this process

- Define the business finical needs
- Define projects available
- Define cost of projects select based on feasibility and profit returns
- Define statement of work for projects selected
- Define project management task based on Program Evaluation Review Technique (PERT) process
- Complete the project organization task lifecycle
- Develop the product organization
- Complete design and development process
- Complete manufacturing and production
- Complete delivery (Dhillon, 2002)

Throughout all of these steps the engineering management roles are filled with individual describes to have the necessary engineering skills. These individuals provided input to the cost structure details.

Compton proposed organizational techniques using system created by Taylor, Gilbreth, Fayol, and Mayo (1997). Following the same methodology described by Dhillon included program management processes, as well as, additional steps geared toward improving the planning details of for manufacturing (1997). Compton suggested the usage of Material Requirement Planning system to manage the manufacturing (1997). The manufacture planning includes integrating supplier deliverables to the production site for optimal completion of part and assembly structures (1997). Compton also includes logistic planning for the maintenance portion of the lifecycle (1997). In contrast to Miller provided no strategic implementations for engineering management process.

Both Compton and Dhillon's approaches exclude the processes developed for new technology beyond manufacturing implementations. The evolution of technology and the movement to global markets is another area exclude in the development of implementable system. The inclusion of detailed software development programs is excluded from the process. There is an application to purchase software suggested by Dhillon in the development of overall programs (2002).

In the articles review system and methods used to manage engineering products or process were the focus. The articles demonstrated additional methods for software estimation and analysis, manufacturing engineering systems, and customer requirements. In event review little detail described the strategic implementation of engineering management concepts. The strategic implementation of engineering management models can aid companies in reducing time to market.

Thriving companies search heavily for that competitive edge. The driving factors to control a majority of the market with their products require corporations to understand their environment. How do corporations maintain market share? How can a company extend the life of a product? How does a corporation continue to evolve a product to beat the competitor to market? Markets expanding the globe force environmental changes, while driving organizational changes and business needs. The improvements of systematic implementations incorporating engineering management philosophies create structured organization needs. Using engineering management concepts in all customers, service, deliverable interchanges demonstrated the data flows and process linkages that may not be obvious. A complete system development life cycle management process drives corporations seeking the competitive edge.

IMPLEMENTATION

Increase company profits, decrease production cost, shorten time to market, and increase product life cycles become the goal of management. Developing the next stage of managers while looking for opportunities to grow the business in adjacent market or maybe establishing new markets. The development of educational programs provided managers with the skills necessary to move product development (Kotnour et al., 2005). The integrated life cycles of both the product and the organization demonstrate the real-world application of corporate development. The underlining objectives of creating lean production entities are a sub-system initiative to high-level management.

The life of a product is the measure of time from creation in design and development until the product is replaced from a customer perspective. The replacement process happens when the customer base purchases a similar or advance product eliminating the need or desire for the previous product. The company that continues to meet the need and desires of the customer develops products intercepting the ending life cycle of other products. In the process of developing product the corporate requirement is to win as much market from competitors drives the engineering and system innovation processes. Engineering management's roles now include Porter Five Forces and Strengths-Weakness-Opportunities-Threats (SWOT) analysis. This process aligned to the development of new products or the derivative of old products. The concepts are integrated as definition one drives the other.

BUSINESS STRATEGIC DEVELOPMENT

Similar too many other entities life cycle processes impact corporations and organizations. The organization environment's cycle is based on product sales and innovations. The Leadership and corporate organization environment develops in alignment to the following life cycle. Ward stated there are five life cycle stages that organizations go through (2003). These stages represent roles required by leaderships in the development of an organization. Ward defined the Creator as the function of developing a new concepts and winning market share (2003). This person provided the mission and goal of the organization (Ward, 2003). The next role is the Accelerator of the organization (Ward, 2003). This individual is aware of competitor and continues to move the business forward by maintaining continued growth and expanding the market share (Ward, 2003). The Sustainer maintains present success of the organization (Ward, 2003). During his term there is little movement in either direction as far as market share is concerned. In the event the organization begins to lose market position the necessary roles is a Transformer (Ward, 2003). This is one that can move the business forward even in the loose of market and drive the corporation back to a growth position

(Ward, 2003). The final role Ward described is the Terminator (2003). The position of the terminator is to extract the value of the past system and create some new of the organization (Ward, 2003). The leadership lifecycle is important to the development of engineering management due to the fact most management of today are engineers and are key figures in the development of new technologies (Kotnour, et al., 2005). Many new innovators in growing industries are engineers. There is a growing need for those individuals to be aware of the roles placed on the positions they occupy (Ward, 2003). Ward's described the evolutionary process of organizations giving insight to leadership's responsibility and position as the guide for the organization. According to Ward,

> How organizations evolve and their leadership needs change as the organization changes. For organizations and leaders alike, it is essential that they be able to identify the lifestage the organization is in and when it is undergoing a transition to a new lifestage in order to change the leadership role and avoid decline. (Ward, 2003, p. 5)

As well studies have shown corporations and leadership evolve in similar manners. The development of the corporations' lifecycles illustrated the stages corporations experience in the development of full portfolios and bodies of work (Adizes, 2004). The stages of the corporations are

- Courtship
  - Affair
- Infancy
  - Infant Mortality
- Go-Go
  - Founder or Family Trap
- Adolescence
  - Unfulfilled Entrepreneur
  - Divorce
- Prime
- Stable
- Aristocracy
- Early Bureaucracy
- Bureaucracy
- Death (Adizes, 2004).

Each stage may have leadership roles engineering managers' hold and demonstrate applicable skills to complete the necessary management task (Ward, 2003). The termination role effectively required a transformation or creation role at some point in the process to maintain the organization (Ward, 2003). Many industries find it necessary to evolve and recreate themselves (Dess, Lumpkin, & Eisner, 2007). Acknowledgement of the life cycle and awareness drive the roles within the lifecycle, which shall be illustrated later in this document. It is the responsibility of leadership to be aware of their role in the organization but also understand the position of the corporation in its lifecycle (Ward, 2003). The ultimate desire is maintain a position of stability and accelerated leadership (Ward, 2003). The internal processes of the corporation should align to these strategic goals (Ward, 2003). The value of managers understanding this aligns to the expanding nature of engineering management as a body of knowledge.

The use of SWOT and Proter's Force Five are illustrations of leadership's analysis of corporate positioning (Dess et al., 2007). The evaluations provide leadership with data on product comparisons and market trends (Dess et al., 2007). The decision to moving various directions for business profits evolve from the market analysis, supplier data, distribution process, and product cost (Dess et al., 2007). The impact to the engineering function evolves partially from data provided by such analysis. Dhillon provided life cycle cost to aid management in these decisions (1989). Dhillon suggested there are environmental drivers required in creating systems (1989). These drivers establish the process required to analyze life cycles cost (Dhillon, 2002). Dhillon stated individuals constructing cost analysis should have the following skills:

- Finance and accounting
- Logistics
- Reliability and maintainability engineering
- Statistical analysis and quality control
- Engineering
- Contracting and manufacturing engineering
- Estimating (Dhillon, 1989, p. 35)

As well as having these skills Dhillon also suggested that only engineers had these skills and would be required in the assessment of the developing contracts and systems (2002). Many of the skills listed above draw on activities established within the organizational life cycle and the corporation life cycle. These attributes are considered skill enhancements to the standard engineering manager (Dhillon, 1989). The alignments of such task again expand the responsibilities of the engineering management (Dhillon, 2002). Dhillon provided a list identifying necessary qualities of engineering managers such as planning, organizational, staffing, communication, and personnel development (2002). In detail planning task management encounters, Dhillon suggested using standard deprecation analysis, present and future value analysis, optimization techniques, and additional business processes to make decisions (2002).

These concepts are agreed approaches from Kotnour et al., Kocagolu, and Omurtag, which expand the body of knowledge in developing engineering managers for the future. The works of Kotnour et al., Kocaoglu, and Omurtag demonstrated the need to evaluate business applications on the development of engineering projects. These evaluations are beyond that of manufacturing planning practices generally completed by industrial engineers. The inclusions of Master of Business (MBA) degrees, which are obtained by many engineering personnel today, align with direction of the global markets in creating skilled organizations (Botero et al., 2005). The skills driving corporation profits draw on core-engineering knowledge defined in the continuous evolution of technologies and product associated with developing technologies (Kotnour et al., 2005). Having capable staff aware of both practices demonstrates corporations on the cutting edge of education and development of their leadership (Kotnour et al., 2005). The cross functional application of these skills allows corporation to streamlining staffing needs for business development. Generally, during contractual proposal development and system analysis two functional areas would need to be represented (Dhillon, 2002).

As educational systems develop to align to the corporate environment so will the skills, developing engineers with applicable business knowledge and skills allow there to be one individual functionally representing two areas (Dhillon, 2002).

The engineering mathematical application for business decisions go beyond initial processes for financing of the company itself. The inclusion of Dhillon's approach demonstrated the systematic steps in evaluating the cost of developing, testing, supplier interfaces, and fault tree analysis of the proposed product for development and production (2002). Dhillon used forecasting method in determining economic advantages to developing a specific product (2002). The forecasting process allows the engineer to understand the demand for the product where further analysis details of optimizations and manufacturing needs are evaluated to develop complete cost (Dhillon, 2002). In the Dhillon suggestion of optimization methods using linear programming demonstrated the profit analysis that for cost analysis of sub-components to products (2002). Dhillon approaches draws on skills core engineering exclude for the system design and development processes (2002).

ENGINEERING MANAGEMENT LIFE CYCLE COST

The evaluations and analysis that are required for business decisions and design decisions drive the expansion of engineering management. In evaluating the system development life cycles of products there is a sub-level linkage to the corporation life cycle, which intern required a level understanding of leadership lifecycle. To discussion this in a manageable format the segmentation of each lifecycle shall be presented in an illustration. The following detail illustrates the alignment of these lifecycle and approaches provided by Dhillon.

Project organization lifecycle. Corporation structures may have many projects going on at anyone moment in time. The management of those projects is assigned to various engineering management or general managers. Project status and project completion report out to the upper level hierarchy. Dhillon's life cycle cost began during initial stages of the corporation (2002). In the development of any corporation competitor evaluations and possible product development establish the market entry point for the corporation (Dhillon, 2002). The applicability of the process aligns more to product development corporations and service corporations to established products. Dhillon stated the five areas to review projects are:

- Marketing related
- Production-related
- Manpower-related
- Finance-related
- Administrative-related (Dhillon, 2002, p. 79).

Further details Dhillon included taking into account an established process for selecting projects using cost benefit models aids in determining product lines and organizational structure (2002). Demonstrated below in Figure 4 is the corporation life cycle, which has the organizational leadership stage illustrated also (Dhillon, 2002). During this stage projects are relatively new and little data is collected in a new corporation (Adizes, 2004). It is also important to note that even in established corporation project and programs may flow through the same stages as that of the corporate (Adizes, 2004). Dhillon suggested models such as Disman or Pacifico provided profit and investment data necessary to justify the development of the product (2002).

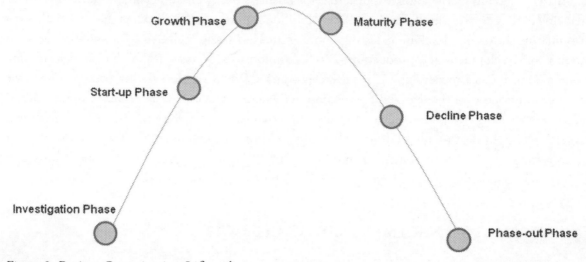

Figure 3. Project Organization Lifecycle

Dhillon includes other analysis method such as risk assessments and more (2002). For analysis of many projects Dhillon suggest using Mottley and Newton Model (2002). The Mottley and Newton model is a scoring system based on five characteristics, which are project cost, product or project completion time, strategic need, promise to succeed, and market gain (Dhillon, 2002). Depending on the structure analysis the completion time can be a driver while evaluating the market share that is captured (Dhillon, 2002). Dhillon suggested for new projects using the Manley model, which provides the profit to sales ratio (2002). In all analysis there may be a need to complete multiple mathematical evaluations based on the position or stage of the project and the corporation (Dhillon, 2002). Dhillon introduced the project organization life cycle, which defined phases projects flow through and require program management processes, project selection processes, and continuous execution (2002).

Dhillon defined each phase as:

- Investigation phase – development of initial requirements, discovering major issues or risk, and gathering main task to execute during this phase such as project cost analysis.
- Start-up phase – stakeholders agree to do the project and selects a project manager.
- Growth phase – staffing up to complete the project.
- Maturity phase – all teams and groups within the organizations have normed and are executing to plan.
- Decline phase – major design risk and issues are solved and organization is executing to finish.
- Phase-out phase – first product delivery (Dhillon, 2002, p. 92).

These phases are an integral part to the development of deliverable products (Dhillon, 2002). The phases demonstrate a high-level view of events that take place in the standard system development lifecycle. Within the system development planning and requirements analysis stages activities from the investigation, start-up, growth, and maturity phases occur using general organization processes (Dhillon, 2002). During the phase-out phase of the lifecycle is executed the system development life cycle has completed design and development, testing and integration, and manufacturing (2002). The maintenance of the product is beyond this lifecycle (Dhillon, 2002). Maintenance occurs at a high-level lifecycle in the system.

Corporation lifecycle. Environmentally speaking organisms have natural lifecycles (Adizes, 2004). To further explain the layered components of the lifecycle process, the corporation lifecycle can be examined from two layers. Many corporations generally have many projects/programs taking place at one time. The successes of these projects depend on many factors contributing to the products lifecycle. The market analysis, product cost structures, and time introduced to market all share in contribute to the success of a product (Dess et al., 2007). To demonstrate this process corporation lifecycle is described as the higher level drivers for project organizational lifecycles, leadership lifecycle and the system development lifecycle. The total impact of the corporation lifecycle can be attributed to one project or program, yet for many industries there are multiple projects occurring at any given time (Adizes, 2004).

The project organization lifecycle has phases that align to the corporate lifecycle illustrated in figure 4. Many of the project organization lifecycle phases take place during the courtship stage in relationship to the creation of projects and examinations to increase market share (Adizes, 2004). The courtship stage is the birth of the organization (Adizes, 2004). Stakeholder commitment is high, as well as program and invest risk (Adizes, 2004). The developing organization can move quickly to the next stage, which is infancy. Within this application the leadership lifecycle activities are highlighted for alignment (Adizes, 2004). The activities of leadership are also included in execution of the courtship and infancy stages (Ward, 2003). Leadership will function in a Creator role see Figure 4. During the investigation of the project the Creator is examining market data for entry points (Ward, 2003). The Creator's results dictate whether there is a need to start-up (Ward, 2003). If opportunities are limited the go or no go decision can be made by the stakeholders (Ward, 2003). With a no-go decision from one product the corporation can still exist, yet when corporations are new to the market and industry that may lead to an affair stage in the corporation (Ward, 2003). The affair stage in the corporation may require a role change of the leadership from Creator to Transformer or Terminator (See Figure 5) (Adizes, 2004).

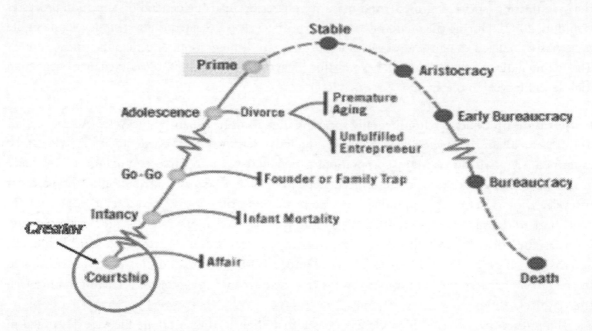

Figure 4. Corporation Lifecycle –Courtship: Creator

Transformer role is one that is able to transform the business using knowledge of new technologies and research data that can expand the portfolio of the company (Ward, 2003). As suggested by Dhillon examining many projects at once allows the corporation the latitude to drive start-up phases of various projects (2002). The data collected from risk and issue analysis contribute to the decision making process. The process excludes the lower level cost analysis of requirement, design and development and testing. Yet, Dhillon provided insight to these cost such as recurring and non-recurring (1989). The models Dhillon provided also take into account support cost, operating cost, up-front investment costs, logistics cost, procurement cost, software cost, production and construction cost, and phasing costs in the areas listed (1989). Even completing a Porter Force Five in the evaluation of suppliers and distribution systems can drive the production cost of the project (Dess et al., 2007).

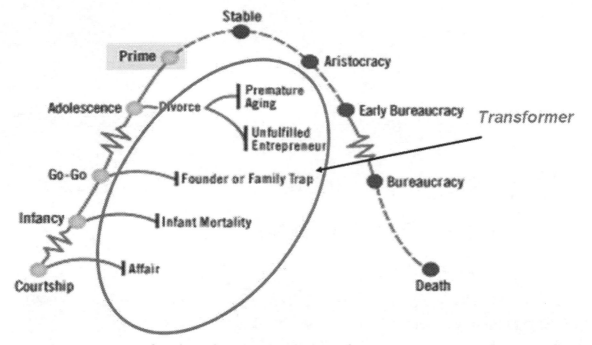

Figure 5.Corporation Lifecycle-Preliminary Stages: Transformer

In analysis, determining plans of execution for correctness is the responsibility of the Transformer (Ward, 2003). In moving to the next stage in the corporate lifecycle the Infancy stage, the leadership remains in the Creator role (See Figure 6) (Adizes, 2004). The importance of this stage is that external investors and stakeholders are committed moving beyond the start-up phase of the project, as illustrated below (Adizes, 2004). The impact to organization development and learning began to evolve more during the Infancy stage (Adizes, 2004). The hierarchal structure should have open communication processes and clear decision making tools. According to Argyris when dramatic change occurs with little communication to individual teams, both management and teams, corporation defensive routines can stall the project moving the corporation into an infant mortality stage (1990).

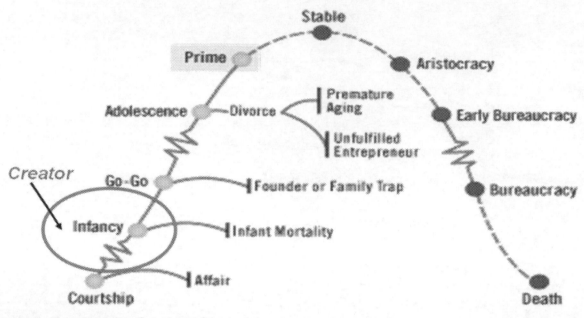

Figure 6. Corporation Lifecycle- Infancy: Creator

The continued evaluations of cost and system development demonstrate the execution of the program plan allowing the projects the move to the growth phase (Adizes, 2004). Remaining in this stage to long may move the corporation to an infant mortality phase, calling once again for either a leader functioning as a Transformer or Terminator. Within the infancy stage is an evolving process recognizing normal organizational functions may slow down the processes to proceed. The level of flexibility of the organization is high during this stage (Adizes, 2004). Open communication and decision making processes provide support the leadership the moving through this stage (Gibson, Ivancevich, & Donnelly, 2009) In developing the organization a system for rewards and detail job designs provide security to individuals within the teams (Gibson et al., 2009). These processes can aid in establishing a system of double loop learning environment (Argyris, 1990). During this stage the project may not have reached full capacity development, yet the continued opportunities to grow remain communicated in the vision (Adizes, 2004). The need to evolve drives the corporation to the go-go stage, where issues and risk have been resolved and market share is consumed by the corporation (Adizes, 2004). During this stage there is rapid growth and sales are high (Adizes, 2004). Many design issue are solved as well and new evolutionary projects are created (Adize, 2004). The Accelerator leader steps into their role. At this point also system development lifecycle cost as decreasing and demand is high (Ward, 2003). The Accelerator uses competitor analysis data to drive expanding opportunities and more (Ward, 2003).

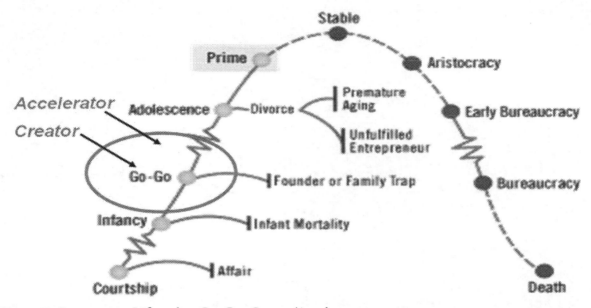

Figure 7. Corporation Lifecycle –Go-Go: Creator/Accelerator

Continued transition to the next stage requires the Accelerator leader moves the corporation to a form of adolescence (Ward, 2003). The adolescence stage may involve the initial leadership to migrate to the next to the project (Adizes, 2004). The process of building partnerships with other entities while maintaining position can assist the corporation in reducing cost the model is described by Dhillon (1989). Dhillon suggested analysis to evaluate make-buy decisions for various components to producing systems (1989). The concept of evaluating distribution systems and supplier impacts should be completed early in the investigation phases (Dhillon, 2002). This provides the adolescences stage with continued evolutions (Adizes, 2004). During this stage the evolution from contract proposal stage or entrepreneurship to structure organizations with management hierarchal definitions began to take place (Dhillon, 2002). In the project organizational lifecycle the product moves from growth to maturity (Dhillon, 2002). The design and development of the product are solidified (Dhillon, 2002). Manufacturing and delivery of product are continued at higher rates (Compton, 1997). This inclusion of supplier integrations are methods used to remove and streamline cost (Dhillon, 2002).

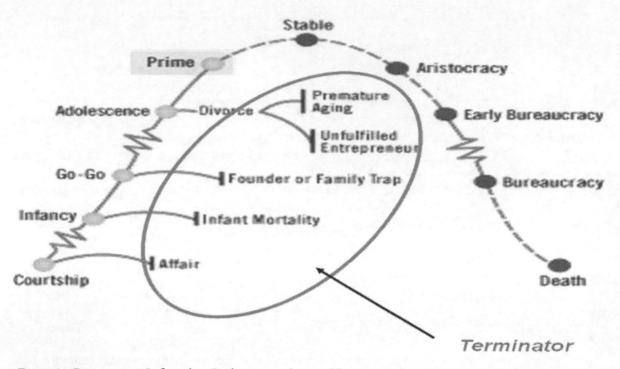

Figure 8. Corporation Lifecycle - Preliminary Stages: Terminator

During these primary stages projects may be short lived when removal of commitment from major stakeholders arise, issues with solution development, lack of communication, issues of budget, or internal alignment (Adizes, 2004). These actions may move the corporation into a dying stage where the leadership role is the Terminator (See Figure 7) (Ward, 2003). The Terminators job requires a dissolve of the company and its assets (Ward, 2003). With a new leadership in place a transformation of the corporation may be possible based on the results of a market analysis and changes to the internal processes (Adizes, 2004). The leadership role exhibited is Transformer as seen in Figure 4.

In the continued success of the corporation the evolving past the accelerator stage and becoming a prime corporation illustrates the additional stability of the company (Adizes, 2004). The prime stage is demonstrated by the consistency to deliver quality products (Adizes, 2004). There are established controls in place for the growth and development of the organization (Adizes, 2004). The development process, as well as many other internal production and product process controlled. The leadership role during this stage is an Accelerator (Ward, 2003). The Accelerator major tasks are to continued market share growth and the assurance that customer satisfaction is high (Ward, 2003).

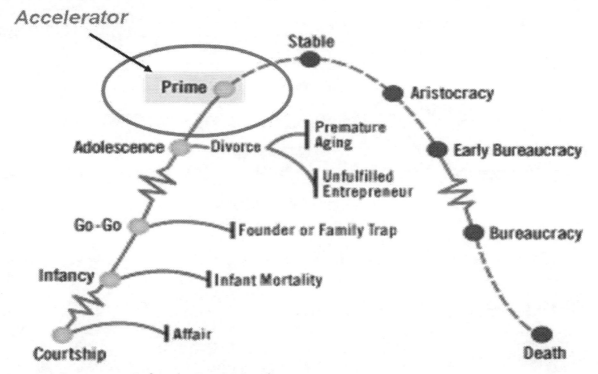

Figure 9. Corporation Lifecycle- Prime: Accelerator

During this stage the corporation missions, goals, and objectives are clear (Adizes, 2004). The leadership of this stage moves the organization to decentralized structure establishing areas of growth and actionable methods for communication (Adizes, 2004). Other activities demonstrated align to control production cost and partnership relations (Adizes, 2004). The stage that all corporations seek is the stable stage (Adizes, 2004). The stable stage can become a point of compliancy, moving the company in a negative direction (Adizes, 2004). During this stage is most important to continuously evolve the company and its portfolio (Adizes, 2004). Corporations must be aware of this stage because leadership can take on two roles. These roles are Accelerator or Sustainer. The Accelerator is observing and searching for the next opportunity in the market, while the Sustainer maintains the status quo of the systems they manage (Ward, 2003).

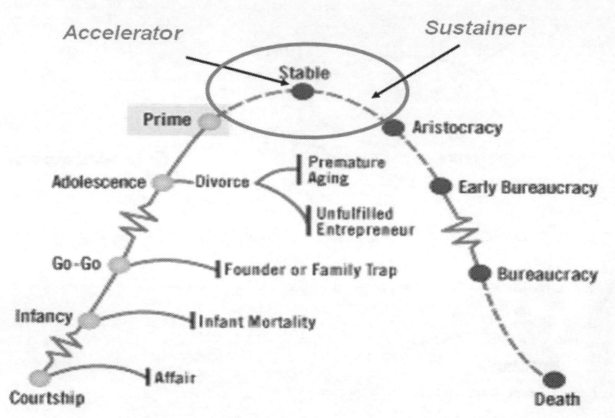

Figure 10. Corporation Lifecycle- Stable: Accelerator/Sustainer

Leadership must always be aware of profit and revenue movements (Ward, 2003). The flexibility of the organization began to wane moving the company to next stage (Adizes, 2004). The products during this stage are stable (Adizes, 2004). This process may move the corporation into an arrogant posture not aware of competitive threats (Adizes, 2004). The next stage is aristocracy where the corporation has position and power within a certain marketing space (Adizes, 2004). The corporation and projects are limited for profit and revenue growth (Adizes, 2004). The acknowledgement of new technologies and lack of additional market entry points demonstrated the corporation perceived position (Adizes, 2004). The corporation has well documented processes and procedures, yet product quality may diminish (Adizes, 2004). Any actions within the organization contrary to the general system processes are frowned upon (Adizes, 2004). Leadership's role is to sustain relationships during this process. The maintenance of contracts and project processes are the focus of this leadership (Ward, 2003). During this stage leadership can take on the Transformer role by extending the product baselines and seeking out new product development markets (Ward, 2003).

Figure 11. Corporation Lifecycle-Aristocracy: Sustainer/Transformer

The control over the organization at this point is limited due to the compliancy (Adizes, 2004). Moving the corporation to a re-birth by introducing the product can force a go-go stage but the influence of leadership must be strong enough to change the organization (Adizes, 2004). Most leadership attempts to become Transformers by accruing technologies if they can develop them (Ward, 2003). This method can be successful, yet, there must be detail analysis of the company being accrued and its opportunity for growth (Ward, 2003). On many occasions corporations in this phase may be accrued by a go-go corporation. The projects during this stage are in no longer growing but are being phased out. The production of products began to end and the search for new concepts begins. The role of leadership during this stage is a major indicator to the next stage the corporation may flow into.

The next stage for the corporation is the early bureaucracy stage, where company partnerships and relationships are minimized (Adizes, 2004). This leaves the corporation in a state of panic seeking new opportunities (Adizes, 2004). These may even lead the corporation to move into markets that are not aligned with the core structure of their business. These alignments are desired to move the corporation to a new go-go or prime stage. Leadership's role remains a Sustainer or a Transformer. In the sustainment position the organizational issues remain unresolved and inter personnel issues began to rise (Adizes, 2004). The process of lay-off rumors drive the collaborative environment needed to reassess and evolve to a go-go stage to destruction (Adizes, 2004).

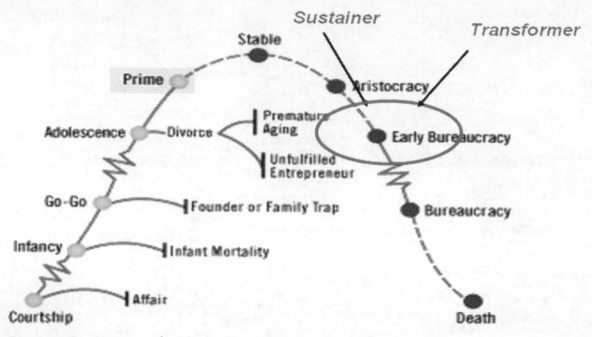

Figure 12. Corporation Lifecycle- Early Bureaucracy: Sustainer/Transformer

The behaviors demonstrated require an environmental change (Gibson et al. 2009). The leadership role as Transformer must assist in this process. The Transformer drives the project organization lifecycles to phases of investigation (Dhillon, 2002). The cycling to this phase in the project organization lifecycle can open the doors to new opportunities.

The next stage is bureaucracy where the profit and revenue has decreased greatly. The projects and corporations have little capital to sustain them (Adizes, 2004). At this point many individuals within the organization search externally for opportunities and loyalty levels decrease (Adizes, 2004). The role of leadership requires a Transformer. The corporation needs an individual that will motivate and inspire the organization to change (Ward, 2003).

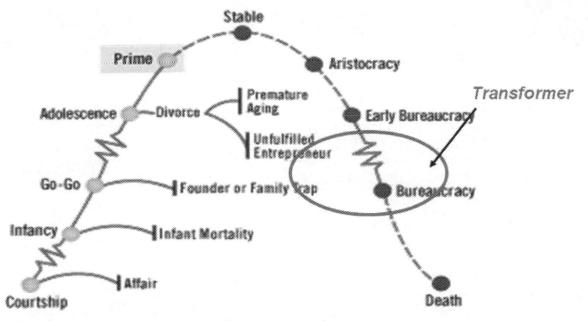

Figure 13. Corporation Lifecycle- Bureaucracy: Transformer

Only a significant action in leadership can move the corporation to a more lucrative stage (Adizes, 2004). The level of bureaucratic structures can be a prohibitor to moving the corporation out of this stage (Argyris, 1990). The need to drive new product development igniting investigation to create new technologies is the responsibility to complete this task (Adizes, 2004). The next stage and final stage of the corporation is death (Adizes, 2004). The leadership role executed during this stage is definitely the Terminator (Ward, 2003). The Terminator's assignment is to dissolve the corporation and position it for re-birth.

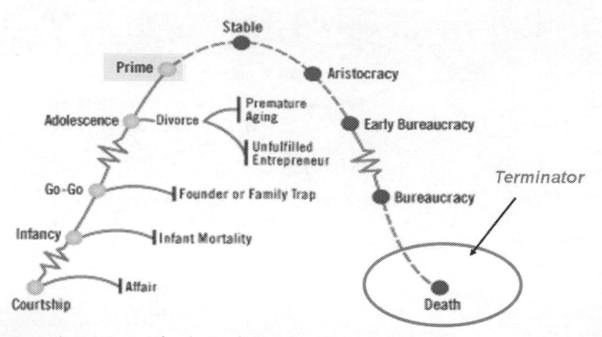

Figure 14. Corporation Lifecycle- Death: Terminator

Throughout all of these stages continuous analysis of product lifecycle cost and product evolution drive the corporation lifecycle (Dhillon, 2002). On some occasions the depending on the size of the corporation death may not occur (Adizes, 2004). Death comes to those corporations with a small employee base and very little external support such as a government entity (Adizes, 2004).

The integration of the corporation lifecycle and leadership lifecycle illustrate the type of leader needed during good and bad times. An awareness of leadership in project organization lifecycle provides a short term and long term strategic view (Dess et al., 2007). The lower level system development lifecycle demonstrates an overall systematic view of health of the corporation (Dhillon, 1998). In many corporations it is virtually impossible for top leadership to monitor the system at all layers of the lifecycle (Adizes, 2004). Warranting the needed for a hierarchal organizational structure aware of the processes and methods of each lifecycle provides visibility into each layer (Adizes, 2004). Solidifying Dhillon's systematic reasoning for using engineers in management positions, this is typically bases on the industry (1989). In many technical environments Dhillon has stated that most management is former core engineers (1987). This is part of the driving force behind many long-term engineers pursing MBA as stated by Kotnour et al. (2005). The alignment of the lifecycles is demonstrated in the table below:

Table 5.

Lifecycle Alignments

Corporation Lifecycle	Leadership Lifecycle	Project Organization Lifecycle	System Development Life Cycle
Courtship	Creator	Investigation	Planning
Infancy		Start-up	Requirement Analysis

Go-Go	Creator/Accelerator	Growth	Design/Development
Adolescence	Accelerator		Integration/Testing
			Implementation/Build/
		Maturity	Manufacturing
Prime		Decline	Maintenance
Stable			
Aristocracy	Accelerator/Sustainer		
Early Bureaucracy	Sustainer	Phase-out	
Bureaucracy	Sustainer/Transformer		Maintenance/Disposition
	Transformer	Investigation	Innovation
Death	Terminator		Innovation/Planning
Death/Courtship	Terminator/Creator		

This table illustrated the transitions between conceptual lifecycles created by theorist in corporations, leadership, project management, and system development. Each position and role has valuable influence of the development of new technologies and new products. To clarify the advancements of projects cost data and market needs are necessary inputs to create implemental strategic plans for company growth.

PRODUCT LIFECYCLE COST

Contributing to the strategic analysis of corporations is the awareness of development cost. Dhillon suggested a detail understanding of these cost as a factor the successful corporations (1989). The development costs of a product are segregated cost from maintenance, and disposal (Dhillon, 2002). Each phase of cost may contribute to the overall corporation cost structure (Dhillon, 2002). The general overhead cost to sustain the facilities and structure of the corporation are defined (Dhillon, 2002). The exception to the rule occurs if there is a need to build new facilities and expand the work environment (Dhillon, 1989). One model Dhillon suggested has four major cost, which are "research and development cost, production and construction cost, operation and support, and retirement and disposal cost" (1989). The equation expression is $Lcc = RDC + PCC + OSC + RADC$. In some corporations some of these costs may not be applicable, yet in developing disposable systems it is appropriate to identify these cost.

Product development cost. Ideas become products and can have opportunity to build strong corporations (Adizes, 2004). The evaluation of cost for the development of a product began with determining the design methodology (Dhillon, 2002). The design method may start in one of three ways; new design from creativity ideas, spiral design from iterative development cycles, or derivative designs from evolutionary applications on previous completed systems (Dhillon, 2002). In each case requirement gathering, design, development and testing must take place (Dhillon, 2002). The variable in the equation is to extent will requirements, design and testing be necessary. In creative development long testing phases are required based on the new development, where for derivative developments this may not be the case (Dhillon, 1998). It is the responsibility of management to understand

and accurately determine the necessary process (Dhillon, 1998). For example to incorporate Lean engineering in Toyota's process their methods prior product selection and market analysis evolve in all three design processes (Morgan and Liker, 2006). The product items align to market gaps and long term strategic business market development (Morgan et al., 2006). This process demonstrates a unique cost structure segmenting the development specifically from manufacturing etc. (Morgan et al., 2006). The requirement and design cost evolve from staffing and organization structure. Dhillon suggested using the following equation for research and development:

$$RDC = \sum_{i=1}^{7} RDCi$$

(1)

Where RDC_i is the ith cost component of the research and development cost:

    i = 1 (product planning)
    i = 2 (engineering design)
    i = 3 (system test and evaluation)
    i = 4 (system/product lifecycle management)
    i = 5 (system/product software)
    i = 6 (product research)
    i = 7 (design documentation) (Dhillon, 1989, p 55).

The sub-component data for analysis are contingent upon the industry of the corporation. The design approach as stated contributes to the details of this summation figure (Dhillon, 1989). These sub-components also highlight areas of risk, which Miller describes as managerial risk approach (2002). Understanding the level of technical requirements and the design method used can stream line the products cost and remove some of the listed items (Dhillon, 1998). Other costs to consider are production cost (Dhillon, 1989).

Product production cost. Production costs are defined as manufacturing cost described by Compton. Compton structured manufacturing cost around specific manufacturing processes used within industry (1997). Product control processes like queuing and just-in-time production illustrate new philosophies of manufacturing (Compton, 1997). Manufacturing planning details when within the production process assemblies will be created and integrated to complete the product (Compton, 1997). All cost associated with this process define production cost (Compton, 1997). Included in these costs are quality processes that complete defect analysis and closed-loop actions (Compton, 1997). Dhillon defined production costs as:

$$PCC = \sum_{i=1}^{5} PCCi$$

(2)

Where PCC_i is the ith cost component of the production and construction cost:

    i = 1 (manufacturing)
    i = 2 (quality control)
    i = 3 (construction)
    i = 4 (industrial engineering and operations analysis)
    i = 5 (initial logistics support) (Dhillon, 1989, p 55)

The sub-component level of this process is also contingent of the industry of the corporation. In cases where the product is software the most important cost in the developing production code is quality (Dhillon, 1989). Generally for hand held items or distributed items these cost contribute to corporation cost (Dhillon, 1989). Additional cost discussed by Dhillon are operations and retirement cost.

Operation and retirement cost. Operations cost are maintenance and support cost (Dhillon, 1989). In many industries this cost is paid individually by customers in warranty and maintenance contracts (Dhillon, 1989). In structuring the cost for customers to pay the offset is profit to the corporation. The operations cost for industries that develop large unit items such as airplane etc. these costs are included in the pricing of the items and can be paid by the corporation's (Dhillon, 1989). In the event there are leasing agreements a large percentage of this cost may be on the corporation (Dhillon, 1989).

The retirement cost fall into the same category based on the product being developed (Dhillon, 1989). The corporation may have to develop means to retire and dispose of items created (Dhillon, 1989). The cost association with such processes may include government entity analysis etc (Dhillon, 1989). All retirement and disposal cost must align with environmental regulations (Dhillon, 1989). These costs are displayed in the following manner:

$$OSC = \sum_{i=3}^{3} OSCi$$

(3)

Where OSC_i is the ith cost component of the operations and support cost:

i = 1 (system/production distribution)
i = 2 (sustaining logistic support)
i = 3 (system/product operations) (Dhillon, 1989, p 56).

The retirement and disposal cost is:

$$RADC = SURC + [\alpha(UMA)(IDC - RV)]$$

(4)

Where

$SURC$ is the system/product ultimate retirement cost
RV is the reclamation value
IDC is the cost of item disposal
α is the factor for condemnation
UMA is the number if unscheduled maintenance actions (Dhillon, 1989, p 56).

The sub-component level of this process is also contingent of the industry product. It deemed expectable to excluded data not necessary in the evaluation of the product lifecycle's (Dhillon, 2002). In the development of products market data along with the summarization of costs assist in determining strategic and tactical steps required to obtain or maintain market position (Dess et al., 2007). These streamlining of cost as well as the reduction of cycle time in that development creates a powerful position in market (Dess et al., 2007). The selection of design methodology and applied standard cost structure illustrate systems using Lean principles (Dhillon, 2002). A major component to the reduction of cycle time is the structure and function of the organization (Gibson et al. 2009).

ORGANIZATION INFLUENCES

The organizational hierarchical structure and culture dictate many of the products initiated. In developing overhead cost for development the systematic implementation of the organization can over price the product (Gibson et al, 2009). In determining the methods required the organization's leadership will make decisions on how to proceed (Gibson et al, 2009). This may even include creating a new organization and department (Gibson et al, 2009). Dhillon suggested the following equation in developing new organizations and the hierarchy:

$$TL = \frac{WF\left(M^n - 1\right)}{M^n\left(M - 1\right)}$$

(5)

Where

TL is the total number of leaders in a company

n is the total number of hierarchy levels in the company

WF is the company work force excluding supervisory personnel

M is the number of persons to be supervised by a superior or leader (Dhillon, 2002, p. 22).

The process allows management to structure the organization as needed based on the product. The difficulty in making these decisions lie in understanding the required out come of the organization (Gibson et al, 2009). Organizational change maybe a need in developing the product based on what design methodology is used, as well as understanding the jobs required within the organization (Gibson et al, 2009). Based on the studies of Argyris it is clear new product development decisions can have a tremendous effect on the organization itself. This is found in individuals that may deem the decision as being a threat to their position in the organization. Therefore the use of organization change models developed by Gibson et al. may be necessary to move the corporation in a direction of profitability (2009). The integration of the lifecycle moves the organization to a more collaborative environment. This philosophy can draw on the expertise of all within the management and development teams (Gibson et al., 2009). The major reasons for making such changes to the organizations are to gain synergies early in the process of design and development, which would decrease the products time to market (Gibson et al., 2009).

The concept of Lean aligns greatly with the structured functioning of the organization. Lean allows the organization to restructure functions for reduce cycle times in development and decisions. Lean is founded on 13 major principles (Morgan et al., 2006). One fundamental principle is "Establish customer-defined value to separate value-added activity from waste" (Morgan et al. 2006). This principle centers on removing waste in development engineering process and production processes providing streamlined and collaborated work flows (Morgan et al. 2006). The general development process has a singular methodology where experts function as silo entities to execute in what was deemed an effective process (Kennedy, 2003). There are generally single inputs and outputs for the development process (Kennedy, 2003). The siloed effect cause delay in solution execution impacting the team's ability to deliver (Kennedy, 2003). The proposals of Lean practices have an overwhelming affect on the silo functioning organizations. In many case concepts of concurrent engineering is deemed Lean engineering when that is not always the case (Kennedy, 2003). Morgan et al. suggested systems similar to that of Toyota's, where set- based concurrent engineering. The set-based process opens the door for an extremely collaborative environment somewhat different from the general process. Making changes of this nature to older organizations may be deemed difficult to implement, yet are viewed some as best practice for reducing time to market (Gibson et al. 2009). An established point of the process is the leadership moving the focus back to what type of leadership roles best align with the corporation process (Gibson et al., 2009).

In any event creating a collaborative environment system that allows a free flow of data and ideas is valued for the future structure of engineering management (Morgan et al., 2006). The alignment of leadership roles, actions, and needs can create the future for all industries eager to develop cutting edge systems. Sometimes technologies and standard processes can be a hindrance.

CHAPTER 5

Let's Talk About It

Corporate competition for market position and double figures in profits drive corporation to re-examine their intern methods and processes (Dess et al. 2007). Decreasing the internal system development lifecycle in an attempt to reduce product time to market are strategic objectives for many corporations. In the same process many companies desire to extend the lifecycle of a product to reduce production cost and increase the return on investment. Impacting these processes is engineering management's involvement of product development and market analysis (Dess et al., 2007).

Engineering management is a fundamental aspect of many product developments within industries. The processes used to control cost and a production of a variety of items requires some type of management. Managers who are aware of the system and how many products are produced, as stated by Taylor, have an advantage of understanding the worker or workman positions (1967). This area of knowledge according to Taylor leads to economics controls of the corporation (1967). This is fundamental creating the maximum prosperity (Taylor, 1967). The position of manager has extended to include management of people and product base. Dhillon's statement that almost 50% of managers during the late 1980's were former engineers demonstrated who and what type of individuals were being promoted (1987). The information extracted from Kotnour et al. alludes to the fact that many managers have evolved from core-engineering backgrounds (2005). Omurtag described the continued growth in the field necessary based on the technical evolutions in the market (2009). Botero illustrated that this phenomena expands globally for many industries (2005).

In reaching these points of leadership in business, engineers have an increasing responsibility to understand product development beyond that of design and development. Taylor suggested that the majority of leadership should be engineers because of the specific training engineers received (1911). Omurtag focused on strategic needs with the educational environment, as well adding process and technique growth in design and development relationships (2009). Omurtag (2009) and Kotnour (2005) suggest in their findings necessary skills for managing the advance technology environments flourish under the management of engineers. The beginning phases of the field from early 1910 to today illustrated the continuous impact of such employees (Omurtag, 2009). Even in the writings of Dhillon, it is clear from the late 1980s to 2000s there were tremendous evolutionary concepts introduce to the role engineering manager. Kotnour's et al. study demonstrated the cross pollination of engineering and business degrees as the go forward method for developing the skills necessary in business management today (2005).

The field of engineering managers according to Kocaoglu is moving into the broden the boundaries of engineering as a field of study including these management aspects and economics (2009). The continued evolution of technology and philosophical concepts demonstrate to manage businesses of very technical foundations requires a different set of skills (Kotnour et al., 2005). The skill of core–engineering or business professionals does not dominate but rather balances the perspective of the individual (Omurtag, 2009). The individual personality and characteristics are both areas of much constant research. The desire to frame the perfect leader continues to be the focus of many. The math and science foundation of engineering aligned to the account and economic analysis desired drive the industrial change (Omurtag, 2009). Even today business students study aspects of operation management within production process (Dess et al., 2007). Preparing individuals for these roles can strengthen the economic positioning of any country.

Dhillon illustrates the importance of program management skills, organizational, and cost structures (2002). The program management subject is key skills to understanding the task of the project (Dhillon, 2002). These processes are the exact same method demonstrated by Taylor in task management (1967). The concept includes, today, more data on cost of the processes. As described by Mizell cost estimating and task details are some of the more complicated items to complete in create a product (2007). Jones even contributed with the lessons learned in executing program management task (2007). A key skill Jones seemed to posse was the ability to understand the product development and production process (2007).

The work of Taylor in creating scientific management for the manufacturing of product illustrates the requirement to understand task management (1967). The concept of task management constructs the foundation for project management and project organizational lifecycle described by Dhillon. Identifying and controlling the task required to complete the production of the product are tactical requirements do engineering management (Dhillon, 2002).

For many years in alignment to Taylor, most focused on the production work of the product. Compton expands the engineering management process by including organizational techniques for employee engagement and employee satisfaction (1997). Compton's approach highlighted the organizational structure and building groups with flexibility (1997). Compton's work described improvement s to product development by emphasizing improvements of the employee experience (1997).

Both Dhillon (2002) and Compton (1997) suggestions for organizational development aligned to the needs of the project. The structure of the organization designing and developing the product maps to the creating the project organizational life cycle of a product (Dhillon, 2002). In the development of the project plan Dhillon's suggest to have functional representation in the process highlights a strategic alignment to staffing needs for the completion of the project (Dhillon, 2002). Understanding the corporation and product lifecycle in alignment with SWAT and Porter's Force Five processes can provide the corporations with certain advantages (Dess et al., 2007). The advantages center on time to market and corporation's positional needs (Dess et al. 2007).

Products are developed and sold to create wealth and profit for corporations (Dess et al., 2007). Being the first company in a certain product space allows the corporation to accomplish two things (Dess et al., 2007). The first of those two is profit. The profit received from first introducing an item to market may be minimal depending on the cost to produce the product (Dess et al, 2007). In certain events production cost may not be a driver rather being the first to market is more important. In either case it is the manager's role is to understand the cost of getting a system to market and maintaining a certain level of profit (Dhillon, 2002). The information provided by Dhillon described in detail the costing practices of most corporations (2002). The costing analysis is from an aerospace engineering perspective. Dhillon reviewed projects from the idea phase to the completed product phase (2002). Dhillon demonstrated even maintenance and logistic processes that have to consider in distribution of the product (2002). The methods used by Dhillon are applicable in any product market from service to system development or construction (2002).

Within this application awareness of such concepts is an advantage to the management structure during strategic planning development and corporations positioning. Depending on where the corporation is in the lifecycle processes may dictate what type of products that corporation should be developing. For example if the corporation is in the Aristocracy stage, the type of leadership needed may be a Transformer and maybe not a Sustainer (Adizes, 2004). If the corporation's desire is to expand their product base or even just the company lifespan then the need for a Transformer is clear (Ward, 2003). The Transformer's role is look for opportunities in product development to introduce something new. The Transformer though must be aware of the development and production cost (Ward, 2003). As well the Transformer must understand the market in which the product is being introduced. Additional the Transformer must be an innovative person willing to take risk, while maintaining the company overall goals and objectives (Ward, 2003).

Dhillon (2002) and Compton's (1997) work aids in describing cost processes, manufacturing processes, logistic processes, and organization processes areas, which the Transformer will have to be involved. In the development of the new product the Transformer can be multiple people, yet the overall goal of the corporation would be to move the company in a position direction with new baseline products (Ward, 2003). The Transformer can use the same methods in developing a derivative product based on the corporation's portfolio (Ward, 2003). In either process the management structure and individuals will need skills to understand actions occurring internal and external to their corporation (Dhillon, 2002).

The management skills desired for each of the corporation stages draw from Compton (1997) and Dhillon's (1987) approaches. The courtship stage is fundamentally described in the project management process described by Dhillon, yet the much of the stage represent work done by the designing and development engineering or individual creating new product (2002). The individual leader during this stage is generally the creator or inventor of the product (Adizes, 2004). This individual is generally aware of the task required to build a functional representation of the product (Dhillon, 2002). This individual although having limited knowledge of production and marketing etc. of the product provided guidance to complete development (Dhillon, 2002). Dhillon provided design methodologies in system analysis to create the most manufacturable and reliable product, assisting the creator in the development of the new product (2002).

As we move through the stages of the corporation lifecycle the application of Dhillon's and Compton's methods are implementable during any stage. Such philosophies can exist at a project level (Dhillon, 2002). The application at a project level illustrates the many stages any one corporation may function (Adizes, 2004). Much of this process depends greatly on the corporation's portfolio (Dess et al., 2007). The central objective of this application is awareness for corporate leadership (Adizes, 2004). The impact of a corporate lifecycle can have on product development selection, organizational structures, and management roles are concepts the management structure uses in decision making. Understanding the progressive process of any product at any level requires a broad view of the product's lifecycle, as well as the corporate lifecycle. All of these items have influence on company goals and objects for strategic growth.

In summary the fundamental concepts of Dhillon, Compton, Miller and Taylor illustrated the functional application of product lifecycles. The alignments of the lifecycles benefit corporations in many industries. Most business schools teach corporate strategic lifecycles demonstrating the relationships within all of the lifecycles. The system alignments are imperative to a company's long term success.

REFERENCE

Adizes, I. (2004). *Managing corporate lifecycle.* Santa Barba, CA: Adizes Institute.

Argyris, C. (1990). *Overcoming organizational defenses.* Needham Heights, MA: Allyn-Bacon.

Bhandary J. M. (2007). Engineering management. *Hospitals & Health Networks / AHA, 81*(6), 8.

Botero, S., & Castro, C. (2005). The experience of engineering management in South America: The cases of Columbia and Peru. *Engineering Management Journal, 17*(1), 9-14.

Componation, P. J., Youngblood, A. D., Utley, D. R., & Farrington, P. A. (2008). A preliminary assessment of the relationships between project success, system engineering, and team organization. *Engineering Management Journal, 20*(4), 40-46.

Compton, W. D. (1997). *Engineering management: Creating and managing world-class operations.* Upper Saddle River, NJ: Prentice Hall.

Compton, W. D. (1992). *Manufacturing systems: Foundations of world-class practice.* Washington, D.C.: National Academy Press.

Compton, W. D. (1969). *The interaction of science and technology.* Urbana, IL: University of Illinois Press.

Compton, W. D. (1988). *Design and analysis of integrated manufacturing systems.* Washington, D.C.: National Academy Press

Dess, G., Lumpkin, G., & Eisner, A. (2007). *Strategic management.* New York, NY: McGraw-Hill.

Dhillon, B. S. (1987). *Engineering management: Concepts, procedures and models.* Lancaster, PA: Technomic Publishing Company.

Dhillon, B. S. (2002). *Engineering and technology management tools and applications.* Boston, MA: Artech House Inc.

Dhillon, B. S. (1989). *Life cycle costing: Techniques, models and applications.* New York, NY: Gordon and Breach, Science Publishers.

Dhillon, B. S. (1998). *Advanced design concepts for engineers.* Lancaster, PA: Technomic Publishing Company.

Dhillon, B. S. (1996). *Engineering design: A modern approach.* New York, NY: McGraw-Hill.

Distefano, M. J., & O'Brien, W. J. (2009). Comparative analysis of infrastructure assessment: Methodologies at the small unit level. *Journal of Construction Engineering & Management, 135*(2), 96-107. doi: 10.1061/(ASCE)0733-9364(2009)135:2(96)

Feigenbaum, A. V. (2009). *The power of management innovation.* New York, NY: McGraw-Hill.

Gibson, J. L., Ivancevich, J. M., & Donnelly, J. H. (1976). *Organizations: Behavior, structure and process.* (Rev. ed.) Dallas, TX: Business Publications.

Harrington, H. J. (2006). *Process management excellence: The art of excelling in process management.* Chico, CA: Paton Press.

Jain, R., & Chandrasekaran, A. (2009). Rapid system development (RSD) methodologies: proposing a selection framework. *Engineering Management Journal, 21*(4), 30-35.

Jones, R. (2007). Engineering projects in the real world. *Engineering Management Journal, 17*(6), 38-41. doi: 10.1049/em:20070607

Karimi, J., Somers, T. M., & Bhattacherjee, A. (2007). The role of information systems resources in ERP capability building and business process outcomes. *Journal of Management Information Systems, 24*(2), 221-260.

Kennedy, M. N. (2003). *Product development for the lean enterprise: Why Toyota's system is four times more productive and how you can implement it.* Richmond, VA: The Oaklea Press.

Kocaoglu, D. F. (2009). Engineering management: Where it was, where it is now, where it is going. *Engineering Management Journal, 21*(3), 23-25.

Kotnour, T., & Farr, J. V. (2005). Engineering management: Past, present, and future. *Engineering Management Journal, 17*(1), 15-26.

Kumarapeli, P., De Lusignan, S., Ellis, T., & Jones, B. (2006). Using unified modeling language (UML) as a process-modeling technique for clinical-research process improvement. *Medical Informatics and the Internet in Medicine, 32*(1), 51-64.

Miller, R. (2002). *The strategic management of large engineering projects: Shaping institutions, risk, and governance.* Cambridge, MA: MIT Press.

Miner, J. B. (1995). *Administrative and management theory.* Brookfield, VT: Dartmouth Publishing Company.

Mizell, C., & Malone, L. (2007). A project management approach to using simulation for cost estimation on large, complex software development projects. *Engineering Management Journal, 19*(4), 28-34.

Morgan, J.M. & Liker, J.K. (2006). *The Toyota product development system: Integrating people, process, and technology.* New York, NY: Productivity Press.

Omurtag, Y. (2009). Engineering management: Past, present and a brief look into the future for the EMJ founders' special issue. *Engineering Management Journal, 21*(3), 33-35.

Omurtag, Y. (2009). What is engineering management? A new look at an old question. *Engineering Management Journal, 21*(4), 3-6.

Sauser, B., & Boardman, J. (2008). Taking hold of system of systems management *Engineering Management Journal, 20*(4), 3-8.

Singer, J. E. (2009). Engineering program management. *Engineering Management Journal, 21* (3), 38-39.

Taylor, F. W. (1967). *The principles of scientific management.* New York, NY: W.W. Norton & Company, Inc.

Taylor, F. W. (1911). *Shop management.* New York, NY: McGraw-Hill.

Venigalla, M. M., & Baik, B. H. (2007). GIS-Based engineering management service functions: taking GIS beyond mapping for municipal governments. *Journal of Computing in Civil Engineering, 21*(5), 331-342. doi: 10.1061/(ASCE)0887-3801(2007)21:5(331)

Ward, A. (2003). *The leadership lifecycle: Matching leaders to evolving organizations.* Atlanta, GA: Palgrave Macmillan.

Waring, S. (1991). *Taylorism transformed: Scientific management theory since 1945.* Chapel Hill, NC: The University of North Carolina Press.